Barry Crump wrote his first [book, *A Good Keen Man*], in 1960. It became a b[estseller, followed by] numerous other books which [... His most] famous and best-loved New Zeal[and character] is Sam Cash, who features in *Hang on a Minute Mate*, Crump's second book. Between them, these two books have sold over 400,000 copies and continue to sell at an amazing rate some 30 years later.

Crump began his working life as a professional hunter, culling deer and pigs in some of the ruggedest country in New Zealand. After the runaway success of his first book, he pursued many diverse activities, including goldmining, radio talkback, white-baiting, television presenting, crocodile shooting, acting and numerous other activities.

As to classifying his occupation, Crump always insisted that he was a Kiwi bushman.

He published 25 books and was awarded the MBE for services to literature in 1994.

Books by Barry Crump

A Good Keen Man (1960)*
Hang on a Minute Mate (1961)*
One of Us (1962)*
There and Back (1963)*
Gulf (1964) – now titled *Crocodile Country**
Scrapwagon (1965)
The Odd Spot of Bother (1967)
No Reference Intended (1968)
Warm Beer and Other Stories (1969)
A Good Keen Girl (1970)
Bastards I Have Met (1970)*
Fred (1972)
Shorty (1980)
Puha Road (1982)*
The Adventures of Sam Cash (1985)
Wild Pork and Watercress (1986)*
Barry Crump's Bedtime Yarns (1988)
Bullock Creek (1989)*
The Life and Times of a Good Keen Man (1992)*
Gold and Greenstone (1993)*
Arty and the Fox (1994)*
Forty Yarns and a Song (1995)*
Mrs Windyflax and the Pungapeople (1995)*
Crumpy's Campfire Companion (1996)*
As the Saying Goes (1996)*

*currently (1996) in print

BARRY CRUMP

BULLOCK CREEK

Illustrated by Kerry Emmerson

Hodder Moa Beckett

First published in 1989 by Barry Crump Associates

This edition published in 1996

ISBN 1-86958-464-3

© 1989 Barry Crump

Published by Hodder Moa Beckett Publishers Limited
[a member of the Hodder Headline Group]
4 Whetu Place, Mairangi Bay, Auckland, New Zealand

Typeset by TTS Jazz, Auckland

Printed by Griffin Paperbacks, Australia

All rights reserved. No part of this publication may be reproduced or transmitted in any form or by any means, electronic or mechanical, including photocopying, recording, or any information storage and retrieval system, without permission in writing from the publisher.

Contents

One	Mutton and Spuds	9
Two	The Dog	25
Three	Woolgathering	45
Four	A Merry Dance	63
Five	Over the Top	77
Six	The Winter	89
Seven	The Holding-paddock Gatepost	101
Eight	The Wandering Wethers	115
Nine	A Fair Price	125
Ten	The Thaw	137
Eleven	Showdown at Bullock Creek	155
Twelve	Miracle at Bullock Creek	163

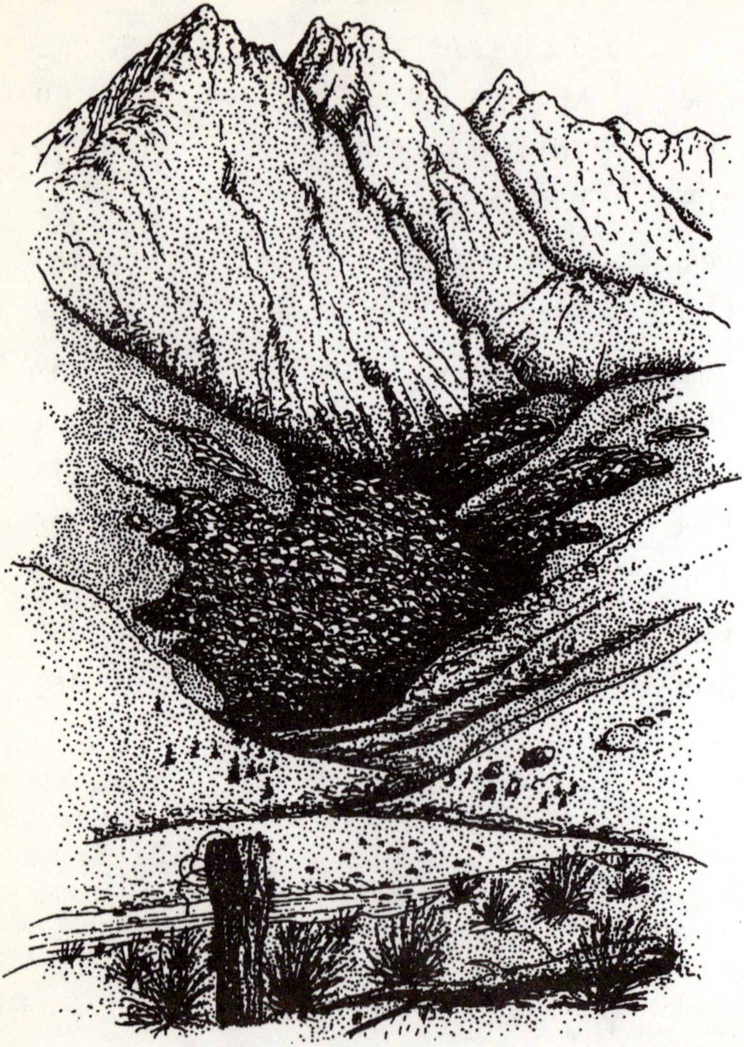

ONE
Mutton and Spuds

Let's put ourselves among the rocks at the foot of a high tussocky bouldery ridge in the Southern Alps, and watch Barney Carter come trundling up the valley in his dusty red ute with a bit of gear under a cover on the back. You can just see part of a stock-saddle sticking out. You can get a look at Barney as he goes past. He's getting on a bit, about fifty or fifty-five, thinnish, greying – an interesting face. We'll keep up with him and see what he does.

He's getting deeper into the Alps now, the mountains are closing in around him, a ceiling of grey cloud across the tops not letting in enough light to even make a man squint. Barney's enjoying this. He's been away for twenty-two years, but he knows this kind of country; he spent his youth in these mountains. He's never been in this particular area though, and he's keeping a lookout on his left for the turnoff to the Doubleburn Station. He overshoots it and backs up and turns off on a road that isn't much more than two tyre tracks in the river shingle, winding around the foot of the hills up a side valley.

When he gets out to open the station gate you can see he's a bit stiff from the long drive. He's walking a bit straighter when he gets out to shut the gate behind him. He stands there looking around for half a minute or so, stretches and then gets in and drives on. The riverbed here is wide and shingly, with a shredded silver trickle of water running through the middle of it, at the moment.

A bit further on the road cuts up the side and comes out on a long tussocky terrace a quarter of a mile across. The homestead and woolshed and some other buildings are set back against the hill near a clump of pines, a dark smudge on the yellow tussock. There's another house further along near a row of poplars and a large bulldozed water-dam.

By the time he pulls up at the homestead Barney's almost decided to take the job here, even if they are inclined to overgraze their front country. The boss comes over from one of the sheds and shakes Barney's hand. His name's Ross – Ross Nathan. They agree on the work and the pay, and you can tell by the way they're leaning on the ute that they're going to get on okay.

"You can use the cottage there and eat with us in the house, or you can use the shearers' quarters down at the woolshed and do your own cooking, whichever you prefer."

It doesn't take Barney long to make up his mind. They hop in and drive over to the shearers' quarters and Ross gives Barney a hand to unload his gear and shows him where everything is. He switches on the power and hot water.

"I'll show you where the storeroom is. You can help yourself to supplies. There's usually a mutton hanging in the killing shed there but we haven't got round to doing one. We've been a bit busy the last day or two."

"Run one into the yard and I'll do it for you," says Barney.

"Thanks, that'd be a help. We could use two of them actually," says Ross.

"Sure, no trouble."

"I'll get 'em right now. Do you need a hand with them?"

"No," says Barney.

Ross goes out, whistling up his dogs.

For the next few days Barney settles in and begins to get the feel of the place. He meets The Hog and young Tommy, who work permanently on Doubleburn. They both have trouble keeping their pants up, The Hog because of his belly and Tommy because he's so thin he's got no hips. The Hog is massive and hairy and good-natured, like a genial drum of concrete, and almost as thick.

"Stick that diesel drum on the ute for us there, will you Hog," says Ross to him one day.

And next thing there's a great crash as The Hog picks up a full drum of diesel and drops it on the tray of the ute.

"Not that one, says Ross patiently, "I meant the empty one."

'Oh," says The Hog, and he drags the drum off the ute and dumps it onto the ground and puts the empty one on the ute.

"You've got to explain things to The Hog," says Ross in full earshot of him. "But he comes in handy at times."

"I can see that," says Barney.

The Hog's wife, seen in the distance, isn't much smaller than her husband, and The Hog is thoroughly scared of her. Tommy boards with them and they reckon that if The Hog's missus can't fatten him nothing ever will. Tommy's twenty-two and he's only been here a few months. He came down from Marlborough to learn high-country farming.

They're waiting for a bit of dirty weather to blow away from the tops. Barney gets invited up to the homestead for a meal and meets Nancy, Ross's wife. Their two sons are boarding in town so they can go to high school, and Nancy teaches three days a week at a little school out in the foothills. She keeps a big vegetable garden going and there are flower beds all around the homestead grounds, all beautifully kept. She's friendly and talkative and active. She thinks Barney's shy, but he just doesn't know what to say. He likes Ross and Nancy Nathan but it's good to get back to the shearers' quarters and make a decent cup of tea with proper condensed milk in it and listen to the radio for a while.

On the fourth morning Barney gets picked up by a helicopter with a woolpack full of supplies slung underneath and flown in to a tin hut on a snowgrass flat, away back in the mountains. The others follow a load at a time, with their dogs in cages at each side of the chopper. By the time they're all there and have their dogs sorted out and tied along the fence and in clumps of snowgrass, Barney has the big tea billy boiling over the fire and most of the food unpacked and stacked on the shelves. And he's beginning to recover from that terrifying chopper ride. He's never been in one of those things before, and he's sure not looking forward to the next time.

Barney's cooking for five musterers. Ross the Boss, The Hog, Tommy, Nick who manages a station out in the foothills, and Alan on loan from Mangatane Station on the other side of the Barker Range from Doubleburn. They're here to muster the Doubleburn wethers off an eighteen-thousand-acre block of high tussock country.

Barney's never been a fussy eater himself and he's not what you'd call a particularly good cook. In fact he's a lousy cook, even worse than he thinks he is. He puts his first meal of mutton and spuds and bread on the table for them to help themselves, and it evokes an immediate and uninhibited response.

"Bloody hell! What's this?"

"Are we supposed to *eat* that!"

"What did your last gang die of?"

"Some doughroaster you've got here this time, Ross!"

Doughroaster – the nickname travels round the hut a couple of times and settles on Barney like a fall of snow on a fir tree.

The Hog, who doesn't see all that much to complain about, reaches over and grabs a rack of half-cooked chops out of the deep panful of rapidly-cooling fat and dumps it on one of the plates. Then he rakes a big slopful of overboiled potatoes over the top of it and begins to cut squares of butter off the pound and fold slices of bread round them. One by one the others do roughly the same, and they eat, with a lot of slinging-off and yarns about station cooks they've known who dished up tucker nearly as bad as The Doughroaster's.

"I never said I was a *good* cook," says Barney, throwing a half-eaten chop out the open door. The chop bone cracks out in the dark; there's a dog loose. The Hog pauses with his mouth half-open to give Barney a slightly hurt look for wasting good tucker and then resumes eating.

"You've got one fan, anyway," says Alan, pushing his plate aside half-eaten. The Hog reaches for it.

The next morning Barney's up before dawn stirring the fire into life. Nick gets up and goes outside and comes back in and says, "Go back to bed, you silly old bugger. Can't you see that fog? It's as thick as mud out there. We won't be going anywhere today."

So they spend the day in the hut, eating and playing cards and reading. The Doughroaster name sticks to Barney like a feather to a flypaper. Before most of them have his proper name remembered they've got to know him as The Doughroaster, as though he's never had any other name.

"Ask The Doughroaster."

"Where's The Doughroaster?"

"Hey Doughroaster! Come and give us a hand here, will you?"

"Are you playing, Doughroaster?"

And they write him down as "Doughroaster" on the score pad when they play five-hundred.

It's a bit disconcerting, but Barney doesn't really mind. It actually suits him to have a different name for a while. And the day in the hut gives him a chance to get to know his doughroastees.

Nick, for instance. A good bloke. Manages a fairly big place out in the foothills, and he's here because he can't get the high-country out of his blood, and he makes no secret of it. You can tell by his talk that his whole life and character have been moulded and tested by his years on the hill.

Then there's Alan from Mangatane. He's head shepherd over there. Medium build, dark hair, knows his stuff. He's made it into the finals of the National Dog Trials twice with his heading dogs. He's about forty and married.

And then there's The Hog. He eats incredibly. An ordinary large meal vanishes off his plate as fast as it can be transferred into his mouth, and while most of the others are still passing the salt he goes on the prowl for more. He gets the roast bone and any spuds or cabbage left in the pots and devours the lot. They've all learned to take enough the first time because there's no second-helping for anyone else when you're dining with The Hog. He pulls the meat into hunks with his hands and stuffs them into his mouth, using slices of bread scooped through the fat left in the pan for wadding. He finishes that off with food and fat all over his face and hands and clothes, wipes his hands on his pants and his face on his hands, cuts an inch-thick slab of cheese to put on a last slice of bread, takes his third mug of tea in his other hand and sinks groaning and belching onto his bunk, to arise a couple of hours later and clean up half a large quarter of mutton Barney has earmarked for the evening meal. The

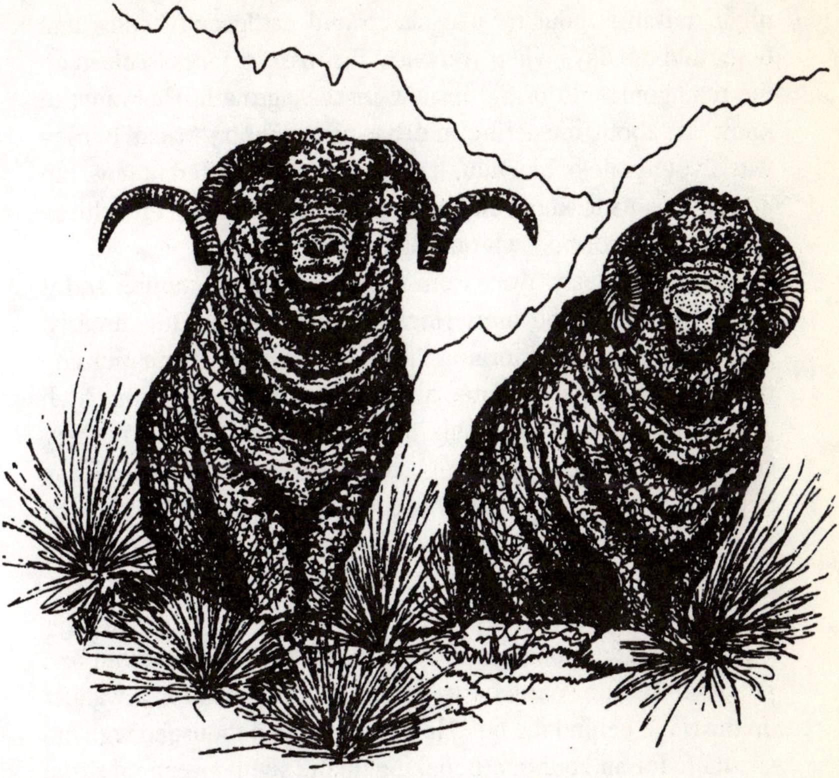

Doughroaster figures he's not cooking for five here, he has to allow for seven at least because of The Hog. But The Hog's easy to handle because he believes in keeping on-side with the cook.

And Tommy, full of questions. He kept Barney up half last night, talking about merino sheep and cattle and horses and dogs, and the days when you burnt the tussock faces to clean up the matagouri and bring on new tussock growth. He wants to know all about mustering and the high-country when Barney was a young bloke like him. It's not that much different now, but Tommy wants to know all about it. He hopes to manage a high-country place of his own one day.

The cloud clears away from the tops towards evening and it looks like they'll be mustering tomorrow. They turn in early. And at daylight next morning the chopper whirls in and picks up the musterers, one at a time, and puts them and their dogs high along the range. Waiting his turn to be picked up, The Hog scrounges around The Doughroaster and gets a big greasy bundle of cold chops and bread to take on the hill with him. Barney wraps it in newspaper.

"Just to keep me goin', Doughroaster."

"Sure, mate. Here y'are."

When they're gone The Doughroaster cleans up the hut and puts two mutton roasts on to cook. Then he goes for a wander up the ridge behind the hut. He climbs about a thousand feet and sits there for an hour or so, soaking up the silent sweeping space of the high tussock and snowgrass country, running back to jutting grey bluffs and shingle slides, with snow still spotted along some of the ridge tops. By the time he notices his leg's gone to sleep he's getting a bit cold anyway, so he hobbles off down the ridge again, stopping every now and then to do some more looking around.

Back at the hut he cuts a pile of firewood and peels spuds and fills a big pot with chopped cabbage for a Hog-sized evening meal. He knows how hungry a man gets on the hill. He's not a very musical man, Barney – The Doughroaster, but he's having a little sing to himself as he potters round the hut.

I'm a rambler, I'm a gambler
I'm a long way from home,
And if you don't like me
Just leave me alone.

I eats when I'm hungry,
I drinks when I'm dry,
And if you don't hurt me
I'll live till I die.

The sound of dogs up on the tussock face tells him when it's time to put the tea-billy on, and an hour later Alan arrives with two hundred and fifty big merino wethers, grey and aloof as the rock they live amongst, and puts them in the yards at the hut. During the afternoon they bring in about fifteen hundred sheep altogether, and the next day they get two thousand more off the other side of the valley.

Merino – the aristocrat of sheep. Men and dogs have to learn how to handle merinos. They'll survive for six weeks buried in snow at seven or eight thousand feet, but if you shift them wrong they'll die on you. Big wrinkled grey bundles of the finest wool on earth, grown on some of the most challenging farming country in the world. The Doughroaster and his mates see only bales of wool and mutton.

They're hard men, these musterers, as hard as they ever had to be in Barney's day. They have the helicopter now to get them up there, but the country they have to work on is the same as it ever was, and the snow and the rain and the fog and the bluffs and the ice ... The high-country couldn't be farmed without these men. It's made them what they are because it sure as hell is never going to change to suit them.

On the fourth day they push a mob of four thousand wethers up the creek and through a saddle and down towards the homestead valley on the other side. And next morning the chopper picks up The Doughroaster and his woolpack of gear, and after a hair-raising series of swoops and banks through the gorges and bluffs that cleave Doubleburn, drops him grateful back on the ground at the station. To the pilot that was just a few wheelies with a light load and only one passenger, but it cures The Doughroaster of helicopters for life. He's never going to get in one of those things again if he can help it. He prefers to be able to get out and walk when something goes wrong.

The next afternoon the first of the mob appears round the end of the upstream ridge, and by dark they're all safely in the big holding-paddock at the woolshed. Ross is pleased. It's been a good muster and the weather's holding. He asks The Doughroaster to stay on and cook for the shearers.

The shearers come and cut them out in four hectic days. They don't like The Doughroaster's cooking any more than the musterers did, but his nickname sure catches on. The Hog and Tommy push the shorn mob out onto the ridges and then it rains for three days solid.

Barney's finished what he came here to do and he's already got some of his gear packed when Ross runs in out of the rain to ask him if he'll stay on and keep an eye on things round the station while he and The Hog and Tommy finish a fence they've been working on to keep the sheep below the snowline in the winter and off the flats in the summer.

"It'll save me having to over-graze my front country if I can get this fence finished, Doughroaster."

For reasons of his own Barney decides to accept.

As soon as the weather comes right, Ross, The Hog and Tommy ride off to spend a few nights in a hut out near the job, leaving The Doughroaster to keep an eye on things round the station. On the second day the weather looks like holding, so he saddles the old mare they've left in the house-paddock for him to use and rounds up the station horses off the flats. By the time he has them yarded he knows the one he wants. He ropes out a big bay-and-white gelding he likes the look of and ties it to a post and lets the rest of them go again.

The gelding obviously hasn't been ridden for a fair while and he's having a bit of trouble getting it settled down. He goes inside for a cup of tea and checks the time and realises he has to lose patience with this horse so he goes out and ropes it and throws it and ties it so it can't move and puts a set of shoes on it and lets it up on its feet again. It's looking a bit shaken on it by this time so he has another cup of tea to let it calm down a bit. Then he saddles it and loads it with supplies for the fencers out the back in a split-sack behind his saddle. It nearly bucks him off a couple of times, but he gets it settled.

The horse is a good mover but it's green and it's lathered in sweat by the time they get out to the hut. It takes two-and-a-half hours, and he's right, they haven't brought enough food to keep them and The Hog going more than another day. There's no one around so he cleans up their hut and puts on a feed of mutton and spuds for them. Just on dark he hears their voices as they come down the ridge towards the hut. He goes outside to meet them.

"That you, Doughroaster?"

"Yeah."

"G'day. What brings you out here?"

"Brought you a bit of tucker."

"Good on you, we were going to have to come in – that's the big gelding! How the hell did you get him out here?"

"Rode him. Why?"

"Hell, that can't have been too easy. That horse hasn't been ridden since he was broken-in, over two years ago! He's only ever been shod once."

"Yeah, I did have a bit of trouble getting shoes on him."

"You've *shod* him?"

"Yeah, they're no good if they're not shod," says The Doughroaster. "It's a good horse that. He'll come right with a bit of work."

The Hog last night dished up a meal comparable in its badness to one of The Doughroaster's, so this one goes down with hardly a comment. After the feed The Doughroaster prepares to leave for the station.

"Everything all right out there?" asks Ross.

"I'd a told ya'."

"Sure. We'll stay out here while the weather holds. We're getting a bit done."

"I'll bring you out some tucker in a day or two, if it doesn't rain."

It takes him two hours to ride back to the station in the dark, and by the time he gets there the gelding's going like a train. He feeds it some chaff and rubs it down and leaves it in the yards for the night. He'll ride it every day for a while now until it learns a few manners.

Barney's feeding eleven dogs they've left tied up round the station and he's starting to notice one of them in particular, a black and white collie with a streak of something else in it, a trace of brindle round the chest and flanks. It's about a year old, a fairly big thing, an extrovert. It comes cocking its leg around the shearers' quarters, dragging its chain still wired to the metal spike that was driven into the ground beside its kennel. The Doughroaster catches the dog and hammers the stake in with the back of the dog-tucker axe, but the same afternoon the dog comes sniffing round the shearers' quarters, dragging the spike on the end of its chain. It's got the idea of working the spike loose in the stony ground and pulling it free.

Now while The Doughroaster can appreciate a smart animal he's not about to let himself get outwitted by a cheeky lump of a pup, so he staples the chain onto its kennel, but a couple of hours later he has to run down and break up a fight between that dog and a big huntaway it's dragged its kennel across to, so he wires the kennel onto a post in the fence and keeps an eye on that particular dog.

After five more days out the back Ross, The Hog and Tommy ride in and take a few days off. One more good go at it and they could have their fence finished and be a lot safer as far as snow goes.

The Doughroaster and Ross are down at the yards having a look at a young mare The Doughroaster's started breaking-in for Tommy.

"What's the story with that dog there?" The Doughroaster asks.

The dog sits looking at them from atop an impressive heap of stones and dirt it's dug up out of a big hole beside its kennel.

"A bit hard-case, that one," says Ross. "I've actually had him working, but he's hard to control. I haven't had the time to put in on him. Do you want him?"

"Don't know. Is he any good?"

"He ought to be. He's a well-bred thing. I got him off Tony Rankin, out of his good collie bitch."

They've wandered over and stand looking at the dog. Barney still doesn't know about the streak of brindle in it.

"Wouldn't mind seeing what I can do with him," he admits.

"He's yours. I've got more dogs than I need at the moment. Glad to get him off my hands."

"What do you call him?"

"He's never had a proper name. We've been calling him Trash because he rips up everything he can reach and scatters it everywhere. The name's kind of stuck to him."

"Well thanks, Ross. I'll see if I can get any sense out of him. It'll give me something to do in my spare time."

The Doughroaster shifts his dog over near the shearers' quarters and feeds it there. He doesn't like the idea of calling a dog after rubbish so he drops the "r" out of it and his dog becomes Tash and never knows his name's been changed. This might have been slightly premature because by next morning Tash has chewed a pair of Barney's pants and the handle of the dog-tucker axe to shreds and scattered bits of them everywhere.

The dog has started training The Doughroaster.

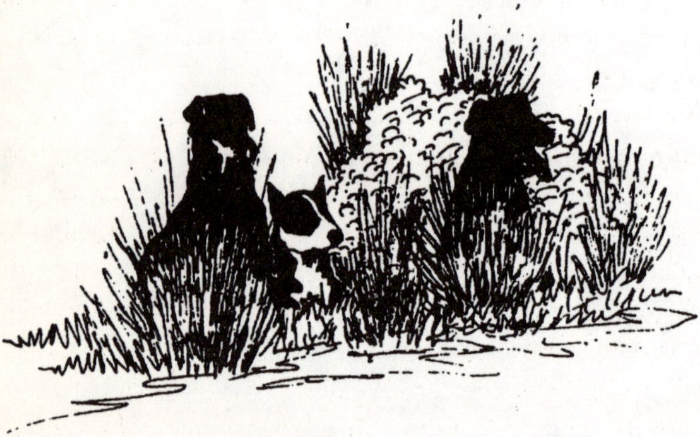

TWO
THE DOG

After a few days round home, Ross, The Hog and Tommy ride out to have another session on their fence, leaving The Doughroaster to look after things round the station. He's got plenty of time to put into training a dog. He needs something to keep his mind off other matters and this pup is just the thing, because Tash turns out to be quite a handful. At all hours of the day The Doughroaster and his dog are out in the holding-paddock practising commands, or working the dog-tucker sheep around on the hillside.

Over-enthusiasm-mad-headedness-is Tash's main fault and much of his initial training is done on the end of a rope or with one front foot through his collar to steady him down a bit. Barney patiently eases the dog into the way he wants him. Tash is a natural heading-dog, but he soon learns to hunt-away as well – a handy dog, and already showing The Doughroaster a thing or two. He's learning something new about dogs every day.

There's still that streak of brindle in Tash, a strand of his rope that Barney just can't do anything about. Like, to Tash, coming in behind means him going a yard or two ahead of the boss or the horse. Barney can make him get behind but he only has to look away for a moment and there's Tash, trotting along in front, in his proper place. Walking behind means that all the scents are disturbed and the boss just has to accept that that's how it is; when Tash is in behind he goes in front. And whenever The Doughroaster stands around talking, his dog has to sit by his boot and lean on his leg. That's the best place for dogs when the boss is standing around talking, and Barney'd have to kick him harder than it was worth to stop him doing it.

Tash also has a loutish streak in him that The Doughroaster associates with the smears of brindle in his coat. He'll do a neat job of heading a bunch of sheep but he can't resist giving the odd heel or nose a good old nip as he hurtles round them. But for all that Tash is getting to be a good useful working dog with plenty of initiative, too much initiative if anything. He's good company too, and The Doughroaster's well-enough pleased with him so far. Ross, The Hog and Tommy have been watching Tash's progress with some interest, and they agree that The Doughroaster's done a pretty good job of training him, but Barney knows the dog still has quite a bit to learn yet.

They're strip-grazing two thousand ewes on the downstream river-flats and The Doughroaster and his dog help shift them each time, but by the time he gets his dog settled down and working for him properly the job's usually just about over.

"You've got that dog of yours working pretty good, Doughroaster," Ross says to him one day.

"He's coming right," says Barney. "Still a bit over-keen on it. What he needs now is work, lots of it."

"The owner of Mangatane's been ringing round looking for help to stick twelve thousand sheep through the dip. Tommy's going over to give them a hand. Why don't you go with him and give your dog a workout?"

"I might just do that. Who's the boss over there?"

"His name's Johnny Knight, but they call him Jake."

"Jake? How come?"

"His initials are J.K. – Jake, eh. He's a bit of a cowboy, but he's okay."

"I might come over to the house later on and give him a ring."

"Sure, help yourself."

Three days after this The Doughroaster and Tommy arrive at Mangatane Station, where there's a whole sea of sheep to bring in and yard up and put through the spray-dip. Alan's still here, but he's leaving at the end of the month to manage a place in North Canterbury.

Their job is to help feed the sheep through from the holding-paddock into the yards. The other shepherds have three or four dogs each, but Barney and Tash manage to keep their flank rolling through. It's a hot day, there's not a breath of wind, fifty thousand hooves wear the ground to dust and stones, the noise is a blur of bleating and barking and men already swearing at their dogs. Tash covers an astonishing amount of ground and still wants to keep going when they knock off for lunch, so Barney lets him stay out there to keep the mob from spreading back out into the holding-paddock.

"Tiger to work, that dog of yours, Doughroaster," one of the shepherds remarks to Barney.

"Yeah," he agrees.

"This afternoon'll slow 'im down."

"I hope so," says The Doughroaster.

By the time they're pushing the last few hundred sheep through the yards Tash is limping, and flopping down in the shade of a gate whenever there's a break. This is when The Doughroaster starts working him harder. He gets him shoving a lazy bunch of stragglers that have been hanging back all day, and Tash jumps up on the sheep and runs across their backs to bark the slower ones through the gateway. When they open up he falls through to the ground and bullies his way back through them and waits for a chance to do it again. This is great fun, Tash reckons, and it gives him a new burst of

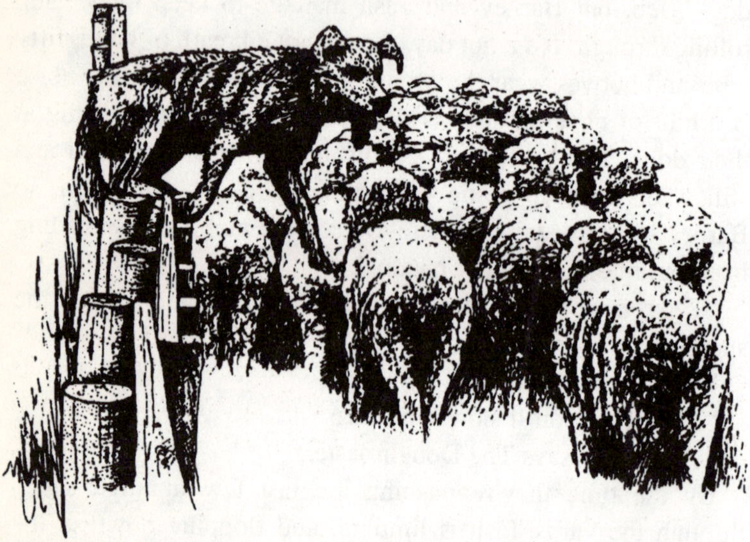

enthusiasm and energy.

But by the time the job's finished Tash is almost falling over, and Barney has to keep him in when the mob is being put out on the hill again. The pads on his feet are worn away and split, and he's run himself skinny in a single day.

"That dog of yours'd work himself to death if you let him, Doughroaster,' says one of the shepherds.

"Yeah,' says Barney, looking down at the bony heap of black and white dog lying against his boot with two half-moons of eye-white looking up at him. "He's been needing a good run."

Johnny Knight is pleased to get his dipping done and he shouts a couple of crates of beer in the woolshed while he writes out their cheques on a bale of wool.

"Here y'are. Thanks, Doughroaster."

"Thanks."

The Doughroaster and his dog have made their first eighty-five dollars together.

The fence is finished, but Ross wants The Doughroaster to stay on and help shear the Doubleburn ewes. He reckons Barney's as handy as a hill-stick to have around the place and doesn't like to let him go. And Barney's easy, he's got nothing else to do for quite a while yet.

They've been watching the weather and when it looks like holding for a few days they get into it. Ross goes off to town to organise the shearers and get some stuff they're going to need, and The Hog, The Doughroaster and Tommy set off to muster the ewes in. They're just leaving the yards on their horses when out of the corner of his eye The Doughroaster sees The Hog's horse take a kick at Tash as he runs past behind it. The kick misses, but Tash doesn't hesitate. He dives straight round to the front of the horse and grabs it by the nose. The horse rears back and the dog lets go and gets flicked aside and the horse gets stuck into it and bucks The Hog off with a great thump into the grass, and gallops off up the fence into the corner of the paddock. Tommy canters off laughing to retrieve the horse and The Doughroaster gets off and helps The Hog to his feet.

"What the hell happened?" says The Hog, rubbing one of his bulging hips where he landed on a stone.

"I think your horse might have shied at one of the dogs," says The Doughfibber.

"Bloody thing! I'll shoot that bastard of a horse one of these days. That's the second time it's tipped me off!"

Tommy comes trotting back with the horse. He thinks it's a great joke. He obviously didn't see what happened either, so The Doughroaster throws a lump of wood at his dog and leaves it at that. Tash retrieves the piece of wood and carries it along for something to chew on. He likes a good chew.

The muster goes off okay. They only have to round the sheep up and bring them a couple of miles from down the flats, which is just as well for The Doughroaster because his dog won't do a thing right today. He nearly loses his temper with him a couple of times.

The shearers come and cut them out in under three days. This should be the last job for The Doughroaster on Doubleburn, but Ross still doesn't want to let him go. He makes out he needs someone to return seventy-one wethers they've drafted out. They've come through from Bullock Creek Station, six miles down the Barker Range from Doubleburn. So The Doughroaster saddles the gelding and whistles up his dog and sets off with the sheep. Ross, The Hog and Tommy deliberately haven't told him about the owner of Bullock Creek Station.

He finds the place without any trouble, in a steep shadowy

valley across the river from the Doubleburn road. He remembers spotting it on the way in and wondering if anyone still lives there. It looks pretty run-down to Barney, the kind of place you're surprised to find still has the power or the phone on. The sign saying Bullock Creek Station is lying in the tussock where a road cuts off and goes a couple of hundred yards to the river. The homestead and woolshed are on the far side, partly obscured by a row of wind-tortured macrocarpas. Even from here he can see that one of the trees has been blown against the end of the woolshed and another has come down across the corner of the sheepyards. The house, the woolshed and another wreck of a shed are the only buildings he can see.

The river-crossing is knee-deep on the gelding and thirty yards across. He gets the dog to push the sheep across and leaves him to hold them there while he rides up to meet the woman walking down from the house. In her forties or so, long brown hair tied back, knitted hat and jersey, overalls tucked into short gumboots, carrying a stick.

"Hello," she says smiling.

"G'day. The boss around?"

"I'm the boss, Lorna Fletcher. Pleased to meet you."

"Yeah – Where do you want these sheep?"

"Where have they come from?"

"Doubleburn. They've been in with our ewes."

"Are you the one they call Doughroaster?"

"Yeah."

"I've heard about you. Well thanks for bringing the sheep over. How many are there?"

"Seventy-one. Where do you want 'em?"

"Would you put them out on the flats past the woolshed there," she says, pointing with her stick.

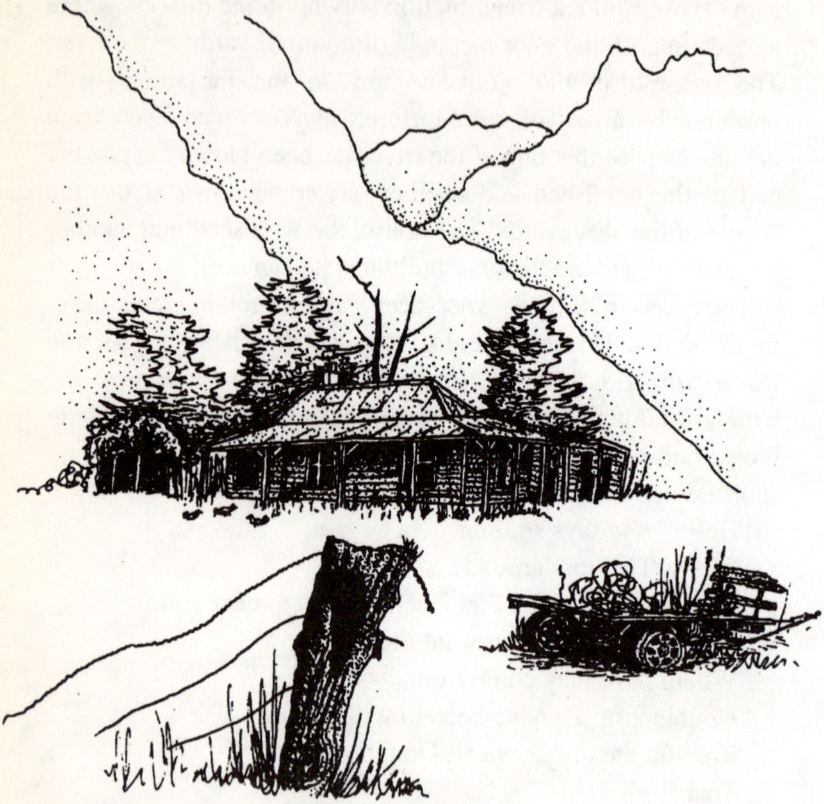

He whistles the dog to shift them.

"Would you like a cup of tea?" she says.

"I could use one," he says.

"Come on up to the house."

He tells the dog to stay put, ties the gelding to the fence, takes off his boots in the porch and follows Mrs Fletcher into the kitchen. It's an ordinary old three-bedroom house. The main features of the kitchen are the old wood range, the open fireplace in the end wall with two armchairs and a sofa round it, a big old clock on the mantelpiece stopped at twenty to three, a radio on a shelf near the window. A kitchen table and chairs are near the stove and sink bench. Some shirts and socks and a pair of overalls are hanging on a rope above the fireplace. There's a big grey cat asleep in one of the armchairs, and a chair and spinning-wheel with a bag of brown wool being spun into knitting yarn. There's a small floppy-looking Bible on the arm of one of the armchairs.

Lorna Fletcher puts bread and butter and cold mutton on the table. She makes a real heavy loaf of bread and the meat's overcooked and dry, but The Doughroaster hardly notices.

"You do a bit of spinning, Mrs . . . ?" he says superfluously.

"Yes, I spin wool for the craft-shop in town. It gives me something to do when I'm not outside and it brings in a few dollars."

"You running this place on your own?" he asks.

"Yes, I lost my husband two-and-a-half years ago now. I've had the place on the market but I've only had one offer so far."

She pours the tea. It's weak. The Doughroaster notices that.

"How many sheep are you running?"

"There's supposed to be fifteen hundred ewes and two thousand wethers, but quite a few of them seem to be missing. I

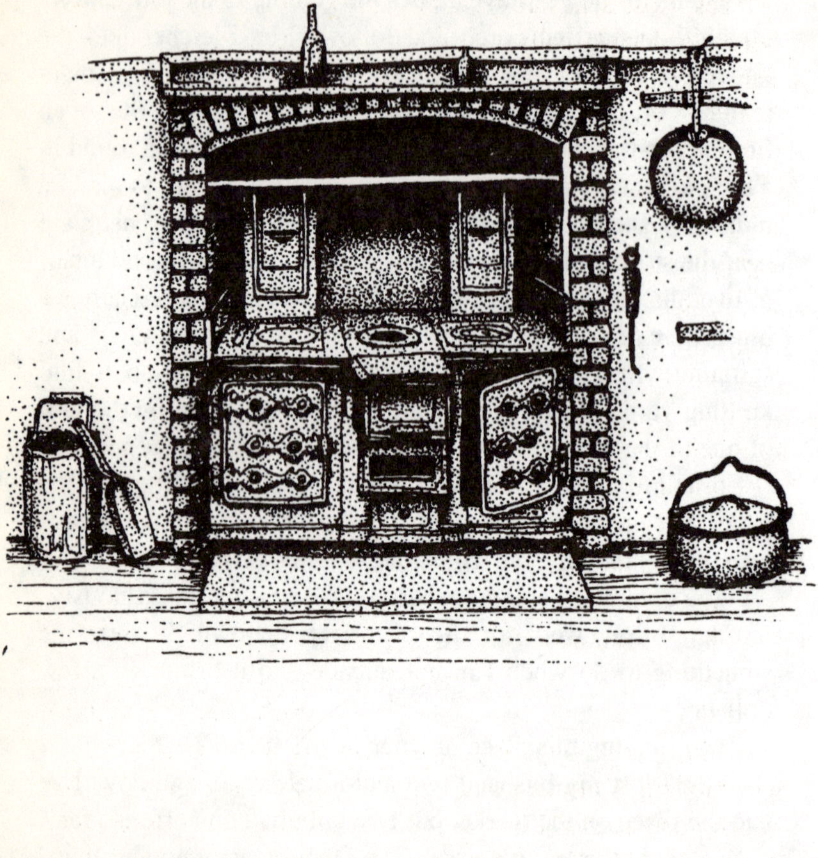

don't know. I'll have to leave them till next year now, I suppose."

"Well you ought to shear this lot and stick them up on your high-country and save this front stuff for winter feed."

"Yes. Ross sends Tommy over when he can spare him. He's been wonderful, really, but he's got more than enough to do on his own place."

"Can't you handle the stock yourself?"

"Well to be honest, Mr . . ."

"Carter. Barney Carter."

"Mr Carter, the dogs I had here all had to be shot for sheep worrying. I've had to depend on the neighbours to move the stock about. I just haven't been able to afford to employ any help. Oh, I'm sorry, I shouldn't be telling you all this."

"That's okay," says Barney. "Who does your shearing?"

"I had one of the contract gangs come in for the main shear, but by the time I'd paid them and the cartage and the bank it was hardly worth it."

"Well there's a few dollars worth of wool on those wethers out there. If you like I'll shear them for you and put them up on the hill."

"That's very kind of you, Mr Carter, but I really couldn't afford to . . ."

"I don't want paying," says The Doughroaster. "I could use something to do right now. Ross has run out of work for me on Doubleburn, I'm just going to be hanging around and I'm not much good at that. I'll come over tomorrow and get started on them if you like."

"Well, really, that's very kind of you. I don't know quite what to say."

"She's right," he tells her. "Don't worry about it."

Before he leaves here The Doughroaster rounds up the seventy-one wethers and puts them in the rickety woolshed to keep them dry. Just as well too, because it's raining next morning when he and the dog arrive in the ute.

It takes him all day but he gets the wool off them. The shearing plant looks like it was thrown out of somewhere else years ago, and the wool-press is a Heath-Robinson contraption that needs two men and a boy to operate, but they get one bale pressed and another half-filled. Lorna Fletcher does the fleeces and the smoko. During a break for lunch she tells the story about the two gold-miners in the old days, fresh from the goldfields of California, who decided to winter it out on their new claim in Boundary Creek, which flows into the river up around the corner there. The following spring a prospector found them frozen stiff in their bunks with most of their supplies untouched.

The Doughroaster, looking out the woolshed door at the rain lashing across the intolerant rock-strewn vegetation of the Barker Range, chews on bread and mutton and drinks from his mug, glances at her and nods.

"It gets very cold here at times," she explains.

"I bet it does," he agrees.

By the end of the day The Doughroaster has seen that Lorna Fletcher knows even less about high-country farming than the people around here realise. Anyone who knew what they were doing would have chucked this place in long before this. Her husband must have been a dreamer to think he could have made a go of it. Most of the high-country eroding away in shingle-slides and bluffs, the bottom faces smothered in creeping matagouri and briar, what river flats and terraces there are have been turned over by the gold-miners in the old days and they've left heaps of stones everywhere, with scrubby growth across them barely enough to keep rabbits fed, let alone sheep and cattle. All the gear on the place is worn out or busted. The homestead and woolshed are stuck right where the wind funnels through the valley from both directions, cut off from the road by the slightest flood, and cut off from the sun by the shoulder of the Barker Range. Wool would have to be worth a hell of a lot more than it is to make a place like this worth farming. No, Lorna Fletcher has no idea about farming, and she's nearly as awful a cook as The Doughroaster himself, but she's obviously no quitter. Just living here would be too much for most of the people he knows.

"I'll come back tomorrow and push these sheep up onto your high country," he says.

"Would you like to stay for a meal? You've been working all day with hardly a break."

"An ordinary day to me," he says. "Thanks all the same but I think I'll get back to Doubleburn."

"Are you sure?"

"Yes, thanks. See you tomorrow."

Back at the shearers' quarters at Doubleburn he runs a bath, drinks half a cup of tea and goes to sleep on top of his bunk. He wakes up some time in the night with the light still on and Tash curled up on the bunk with him. He's even forgotten to feed his dog. He kicks the dog off the bed and gets into his sleeping-bag and goes back to sleep.

He's up early, soaks away some of yesterday's stiffness in a fresh bath, feeds his dog and himself, and arrives back at Bullock Creek soon after daylight, glad to have something to do.

He takes the wethers up the ridge behind the homestead and

spends a couple of hours on the tops having a look round. Back at the homestead Lorna Fletcher invites him in for a feed of cold mutton and bread and tea. The mutton's a bit undercooked this time but he's hungry and enjoys it.

"You've got quite a few unshorn sheep running around up on your high stuff," he tells her.

"Yes, I know. There must be hundreds of them."

"Who does your mustering?"

"Friends from Garston did it last time but we had a lot of trouble with the weather and they had to go back. We only got eleven hundred of the ewes and sixteen hundred wethers"

The Doughroaster calculates. "That's eight hundred sheep short. No wonder your wool cheque was a bit light. All your profit must be running around up there on the hill."

"To be honest with you, Mr Carter, I really don't think it's worth trying with this place any more."

"I believe that, but why?"

"The mortgage payments are due in two weeks time and I just haven't got the money to cover them. It's as simple as that. I've already had letters about a mortgagee sale."

"How much do you owe them?"

"The mortgage payments are two-and-a-half thousand dollars, and I owe the bank eighteen hundred that has to be paid this month. And then there's the monthly payments on my wagon. If they take that off me I'll be stranded altogether. So you can see it's pretty hopeless."

"I wouldn't say that," says The Doughroaster. "You're a long way from broke yet."

"I don't see how."

"Well you've got about two thousand dollars' worth of wool sitting out in the shed. If we can muster in some of your woollies and make up another bale we could just about cover what you owe."

"I couldn't ask you to do that," she says. "You've been far too good as it is."

"Well they've finished with me on Doubleburn and I've got nothing to do for the rest of the year. I'll help you run this place through the winter, if you like."

"Oh Mr Carter," she says, "I only wish I could afford it."

"I need work more than I need pay," says Barney.

"The winters here can be very hard," she tells him.

"I know."

"Well as long as you don't mind waiting for your pay until the station's sold I'd be more than pleased to have you."

"You'd have to give me a free hand with the stock."

"Of course. You can manage the station."

"You've got a deal."

They shake hands.

"What's first, Boss?" she says, smiling.

"I'd better have a look around the property and learn the boundaries and see what we've got here."

"When?"

"Tomorrow morning, if it's not raining."

He gets a bit of a ribbing when he tells them on Doubleburn that he's taken over managing Bullock Creek. He can see they don't think he'll last long, but they're on his side.

Ross tells him that Bullock Creek used to be a run-off for Doubleburn, but they'd had to sell it off a few years ago because it was uneconomic. And the Fletchers bought it and they've had to be more-or-less nursed along ever since.

"If you need anything just let's know," Ross tells him, as he hands him his pay cheque.

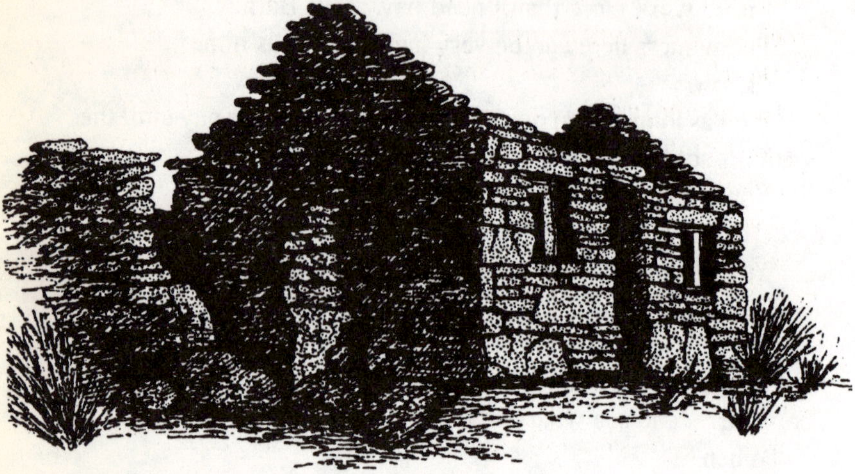

"I think I can handle most of what needs to be done, but thanks, Ross."

"Give us a ring if you need a hand with anything," says Tommy.

"Thanks, Tommy."

"Where are you going to sleep?" says The Hog.

"She's doing up a room for me off the veranda," he tells him.

And she is. When he arrives at Bullock Creek with his gear on the ute she shows him into the old room she calls the sunporch at the end of the veranda. It's got a bed, a locker, a mat on the floor, some magazines, hangers for his clothes, electric light – The Doughroaster'll be okay in here. There's faded chequered curtains on the windows; he leaves them permanently drawn and moves his small amount of gear in. Her bedroom seems to be out the back of the house somewhere.

His new boss shows him over some of the station on horseback. She rides a black mare she calls Miranda and The Doughroaster's on the Doubleburn gelding. Tash trots along in front. Up the Boundary Creek end of the flats there's an old miners' hut, broken down now by rain and frost into a square heap of overgrown rocks and slabs, only parts of the walls still hanging together.

"That's why it's called Miners' Flat," Lorna explains.

The Doughroaster sits on his horse looking at the mean unmade countryside around them and shakes his head and spits.

"They musta' done it hard in them days," he says.

They follow the old water-race up Boundary Creek and try to get a count of the cattle, but they're too scattered through the boulders and scrub. You can only get a horse the first half-hour or so up the creek. Lorna points out where part of their boundary is and they turn back. Some of the western boundary is fenced, but the main boundary between Bullock Creek and Doubleburn is a thousand-foot bastion of overhanging bluffs, jutting out from the weather-broken flanks of the Barker Range.

After lunch they ride up Bullock Creek valley itself. If The Doughroaster had been silly enough to hope that Bullock Creek was going to open out into grassy flats or grazing faces he would have been disappointed. It's a narrow gorgy valley that only gets narrower and gorgier. Only the creekbed is horsable, picking your way among strewn boulders and shattered slabs of schist. A few scrubby-looking merinos are scattered here and there, foraging for a feed among the rock.

Less than an hour up the valley their way is blocked by a huge fall of rock that's come down just recently. They sit on their horses looking up at the towering escarpments of rock around them. A small mob of weedy-looking goats scampers across the face above them with a rattle of dislodged stones.

"This is it, eh," says The Doughroaster.

"You never could get much further than this on horseback."

"She'd be a bastard to muster," he says.

"Don't swear. The sheep don't seem to do quite so well up here."

"The only thing that'd do well around here," says The Doughroaster with feeling, "is something cold-blooded that eats rock."

They ride back to the main valley and pick their way down the flats to Bullock Creek's eastern boundary, an impassable ravine that cuts across the flats from a waterfally gorge split into the side of the range. Everything horsable on Bullock Creek's twenty thousand acres could be ridden in less than four hours.

During the ride he finds out all he needs to know about his new boss; came from Southland, married a bloke from

Canterbury. They took over Bullock Creek four years ago from a background of dairy-farming and raising fat-lambs. They never had any kids but they'd been hoping to adopt one, or maybe even two, when the accident happened.

"We were just starting to get the station together when I lost Bruce," she tells him.

"What happened to him?" he asks her.

"He was driving part-time for Hillfreight to bring in a bit of extra money. His truck went off the road over at Tarras and he was killed."

"That's too bad."

"My family wants me to go back to Mataura and stay with them, but I want to stick with the station till it's sold. Then I'll probably move away somewhere else and start again."

"Good idea," grunts The Doughroaster absently.

He can see now what he's taken on. She hasn't sold off any of her hoggets, and now you couldn't give them away, even if you could fatten them. Ross, The Hog and Tommy did her docking last time, probably because they couldn't bear the thought of a thousand Bullock Creek rams running around the district. Now there's twice as much stock on the place as there should be, and all the ewe-hoggets are in-lamb. Unless something's done about it a lot of sheep are going to die on Bullock Creek this coming winter. There just isn't the feed here to keep them alive.

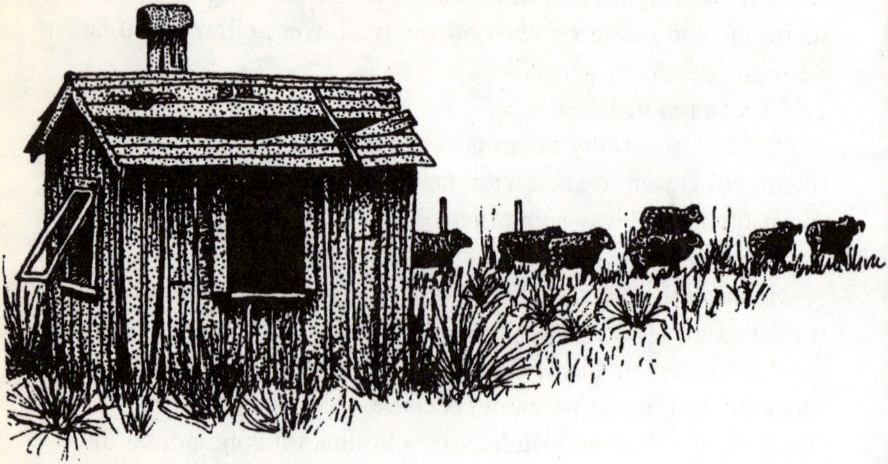

THREE

Woolgathering

The first day on the job the new manager of Bullock Creek Station gets eighteen ewes and four wethers, all unshorn, off the scrubby faces upstream from the homestead. The day after that he brings thirty-seven of them down out of a rocky basin at the head of Boundary Creek. And sixteen the next day out of Bullock Creek. By the time Tash is getting the message that he only wants the woolly ones he has enough of them to make up the extra bales of wool. It's taken him a week because of two wet days.

He shears them and lets them back out on the hill and winds up with four bales of wool pressed and ready for town, which takes two trips in the ute.

The wool-buyer is a sharp little chap who rips him off handsomely because he can't produce a tax number. He walks out of there with a cheque for $3,400. Lorna Fletcher needs $3,750, so he makes it up to four thousand dollars with a cheque of his own and pays it into her account. It's well worth it to Barney to have something to do, a challenge to keep his mind off other things, and he can always get his money back with another bale of wool.

He buys a few things they need on Bullock Creek, like food and horseshoes, gets his dog innoculated for distemper and parvo at the veterinary centre and sets off for home eating a mince pie. That's enough town for The Doughroaster.

He's not quite ready for what happens when he gets the deposit-slip out of his pocket and puts it on the kitchen table in front of Lorna. She picks it up and reads it and starts to weep, saying, "You've saved the station, Barney," and stuff like that, so The Doughroaster finds something to do down the woolshed for a while.

The unshorn sheep left on Bullock Creek will have to be done soon or they'll be too vulnerable to early snow. There's a bunch of horses running on the place, but nothing The Doughroaster likes the look of, so he borrows the Doubleburn gelding. And it's hard work. He rides as far as he can and then it's a two-hour climb just to get up onto the tops, and he and his dog rake through the basins and cliffs along the Barker Range, gathering together bunches of unshorn sheep and hunting them down into the valley and holding them in the only sheep-proof paddock on the station. He has to be careful not to overwork the dog, and the days when it's raining or the tops are fogged-in are welcome rests for Tash's feet and ribs. He's hard to keep condition on when he's working.

By the time they've covered all the workable country they've got four hundred and fourteen full-fleeced sheep in the yards, and the dog's hip-bones and ribs are sticking out and his feet are painful to watch him try and walk on. The Doughroaster sticks him on the chain, but a bit later he sees him hobbling up to the house behind Lorna to be put on a sack on the porch and fed up on powdered milk and mutton scraps. She's a bit soft on dogs.

He borrows The Hog and Tommy to help him shear them and they end up with eight bales of wool pressed and ready for sale. Bullock Creek is solvent for the next few months. It even feels different round here now.

It's a week by the time Tash's feet are coming right and he's looking a bit less gaunt and embarrassing, and by this time The Doughroaster's getting a bit restless.

"There's quite a few dead sheep lying around up on the tops," he tells Lorna, "but I figure there's still two hundred and fifty or three hundred sheep missing off this place. What's the station on the other side of the range from here?"

"Mangatane," she tells him.

"Oh yeah, I've worked there. Johnny Knight owns it, doesn't he? The bloke they call Jake."

"Yes, that's right."

"What's he like to deal with? I haven't had much to do with him."

"Nor me. I've only met him a few times. He came over about a year ago and made me an offer for this place. I thought he must have been joking. I'd have ended up owing money if I'd accepted his price. He didn't even say goodbye, he just drove off and I haven't seen him since."

"Well there's at least one place up on the top where the stock could be getting through onto his place. We might as well have the wool off them as him. I think I'll take a drive round and see him tomorrow. I wouldn't be surprised if there's quite a few of our sheep over there."

It's eleven miles round to Mangatane Station from Bullock Creek and you can't miss it because the road ends there. And it's everything Bullock Creek isn't: fences all tight, proper wooden gates, buildings well-maintained and painted. The woolshed's a mile back from the road and the homestead is on a rise surrounded by trees two hundred yards away. It looks like there's another house further round. Mangatane's seventy thousand acres are on the northern side of the range. You couldn't blame stock for wandering off the cold barren slopes on the Bullock Creek side onto these easy sunny faces.

Johnny Knight and one of his men are welding up some

framework outside the implement shed down near the road gate when Barney drives up. Johnny closes the door of the shed and then strolls over and leans on the ute. He's a big good-looking bloke, about thirty, dressed in western-style gear, and walks around like someone who's used to having his own way in everything. He tips his big hat back and treads on a cigarette he's been smoking.

"Well, well," he says. "It's the Doughroaster himself. What brings you over this way?"

"I'm trying to track down two or three hundred sheep missing off Bullock Creek."

The Doughroaster sees the unguarded flicker cross Jake's eyes.

"What makes you think they're over here?"

"It's just about the only place they can be. We've already done Doubleburn and they're not there."

"What do you expect me to do about it?"

"Well if they are on your place you'll find them when you do your main shear, won't you?"

"We've got more to do here than check for bloody strays off Bullock Creek, mate."

"Then you'll probaby be taking quite a bit of Bullock Creek wool," The Doughroaster says.

"If we do it will have been grown on Mangatane grass. You're wasting your time over there anyway. I offered the silly old bat more for the place than it's worth and if she doesn't want to take it she deserves to go under. The place has had it and she knows it."

"What do you want the place for if it's so had-it?"

There's that flicker in Jake's eye again.

". . . Wether-blocks. Look Doughroaster, why don't you stick to your cooking and leave the farming to someone who knows what they're doing. If you're stuck for a job I could probably fit you in here. You could milk the cows and do the garden, give The Culprit a hand round the place."

"No thanks."

"At least you'd get paid."

"Thanks all the same, Jake, but I'm a bit busy on Bullock Creek just now."

"Well please your bloody self, you silly old bugger, it's your funeral. But don't say you weren't warned. You can do what you like on Bullock Creek but it won't make any difference. I happen to know the place is bankrupt."

"That a fact."

"Yeah. And you can keep the hell off Mangatane. I don't want anyone scattering the stock before we muster. Now bugger off, we're busy."

The Doughroaster drives away from there wondering what Jake's so up-tight about. And by the time he gets back to Bullock Creek he's decided to have a go at finding out.

"How did you get on with Johnny Knight today?" asks Lorna.

"Pretty good," he tells her. "I think we'll be able to get our stock sorted out."

"That's nice."

For two weeks The Doughroaster works on a horse-track up the ridge behind the Bullock Creek homestead. He has to hack the rock away in places and build it up in others. If he'd known how difficult it was going to be he might not have started it. One outcrop of rock takes a whole day to pick away at so he can get his horse past. He's seriously thinking of giving it away when the ridge starts to ease off towards the top of the range. It's still very steep and tricky in places, and he puts in two more days

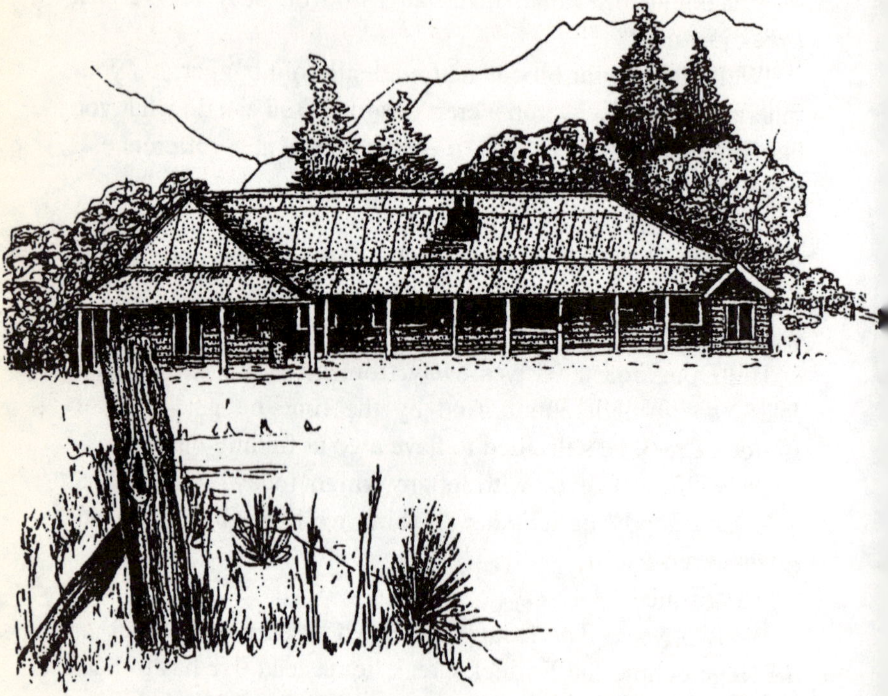

straightening out the worst of them. But when it's finished it's been worth it. Now he can ride the Doubleburn gelding from the Bullock Creek homestead to the top of the range in an hour and twenty minutes. It's the first time there's ever been a horse up here among the crumbling domes and spires on the crest of the Barker Range, but The Doughroaster's not concerned with making history. He wants to find out about that flicker in Johnny Knight's eyes when he asked him about the sheep missing off Bullock Creek.

Four times he rides up here and ties his steaming horse to the remains of a standard-and-netting fence that's been strung years ago across the saddle in the top of the range. He moves around the Mangatane country, glassing the bunches of sheep in the high basins and on the lower faces until he knows all the country and all that's on it. One rainy day he drops right down into a grassy valley behind Mangatane homestead and has a good look over the cattle. He can tell by just looking at them that some of these cows weren't bred on this place. He can see the Bullock Creek Hereford bull in them, and yet they've all got the Mangatane cloverleaf earmark punched in over the Bullock Creek T, in the wrong part of the ear. It's clumsy. He picks out eighteen Bullock Creek-bred cows, all feeding calves with Mangatane earmarks.

Back on top of the range The Doughroaster jams his hill stick into a crevice and sits against the rock keeping his hands warm on his dog, and he looks down across the rainy brown-paper ridges of Mangatane and has a long think. There's two hundred-odd Bullock Creek ewes down there among theirs, and thirty-six head of Bullock Creek cattle. There's at least forty Doubleburn sheep and four Doubleburn shorthorn steers as well.

Jake's been padding out his wool clip with his neighbour's wool and his lambing percentages with his neighbour's lambs and flogging thousands of dollars worth of his neighbour's beef, mostly off Bullock Creek. And The Doughroaster decides he doesn't like it. He stands and leans on his hill stick.

"We might have to do something about this bloke," he mutters.

The Hog and Tommy on their way out to the pub in the Doubleburn ute call in and talk The Doughroaster into coming with them. They have a good time over a few jugs of beer and games of pool with some other local farming people. The Hog drinks jug for glass with his mates and flogs a Jim Reeves record on the jukebox in the corner.

The Hog and Tommy are off over to Mangatane in a few days time to start their main shearing muster if the weather holds, them and two other blokes who are coming over from a goldclaim on the coast to help. This piece of information is most interesting to The Doughroaster, but he doesn't show it.

"Why don't you come with us, Doughroaster?" says Tommy. "You could give your dog a good workout. Jake's looking for musterers."

"Nar, don't think so," says The Doughroaster. "I wouldn't mind but I've got a fair bit to get done on Bullock Creek just now."

They drop him off at the crossing in high spirits, The Hog's actually trying to sing, but The Doughroaster's thoughtful as he wades the river and sits on a rock to put his boots back on.

The following night is perfect for him. Moonlit, cloudy and blowing a gale from the south-west. After the mutton and spuds The Doughroaster says goodnight to Lorna and turns in early, puts on his warmest coat and sneaks down to the shed where he's got the Doubleburn gelding waiting. He makes sure Tash is with him and leads the horse quietly away from the homestead and then he gets on and boots it up the ridge in record time. Horses go good in the wind, and there's plenty of that around tonight. He ties the blowing sweating animal to the broken fence and takes the dog down onto Mangatane country.

He knows exactly where to look for them and within an hour or so he has quite a few bunches of sheep rounded up out of a high basin and headed up towards the saddle in the top of the range. The wind sweeping through the snowgrass in the moonlight makes it seem like walking waist-deep in a silver rippling sea, and the barking of the dog is broken up and carried away in a few yards. The Doughroaster can't see Tash most of the time but he can tell where he's working by the movement of the bunches of gathering sheep up the slope and the scraps of barking that come his way. They're hard to shift in the wind and keep stopping in the shelter of rocks and hollows and the dog is busy keeping them moving.

By the time he has them stringing up the last bit of a ridge and round into the saddle The Doughroaster's a bit disconcerted to discover that he's taken more of them than he meant to. He'd only wanted two or three hundred, but he has what looks like four or five hundred of them. He manages to cut out a few bunches and keep the dog away from them, but he stills takes more than four hundred Mangatane wethers through onto Bullock Creek. He unties the gelding and leads it down his track to the station, pushing the mob in front of him. By one o'clock in the morning he has them safely hidden away in the woolshed. He cuts down a hunk of mutton and throws it to Tash and goes to bed.

He's a bit late getting up next morning but on his way down

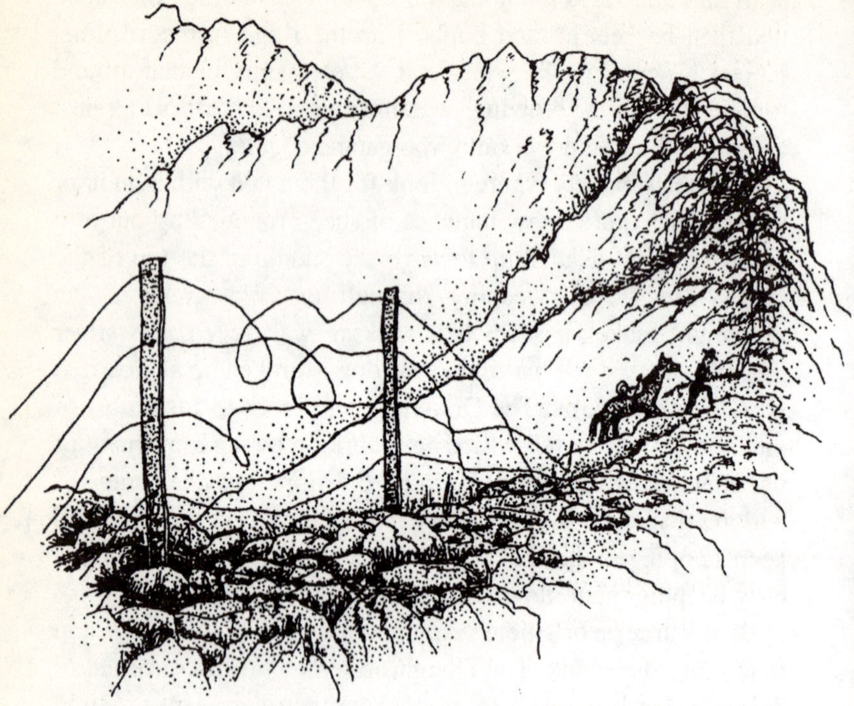

to the shed he wakes up with a start. Tash is sitting out in the woolshed paddock holding about sixty Mangatane wethers at the gate, in plain view of anyone going up the road across the river. The blasted dog's gone all the way back over the range to Mangatane and brought the sheep he left behind on purpose. He's done this sort of thing a couple of times before, but not on this scale. And The Doughroaster's furious. He gets the sheep hidden out of sight in the shed with the others and ties Tash up and feeds him. He's worn the pads of his feet so badly on the rocks that he can't even limp properly, and he's run himself bony. It's quite serious for The Doughroaster, this. He won't be able to work the dog for days and he might need him in a hurry. He's got more Mangatane sheep than he can comfortably handle and there's no way he can put them back without his dog.

Lorna gets a bit indignant on The Doughroaster when she sees what he's gone and done to his dog again. She takes Tash up to the house and mixes up warm powdered milk for him and puts him on his sack on the porch. Tash laps this up he's got Lorna properly conned. He knows just how to sit, with his head tilted sideways and one front paw reaching out to touch her, to get anything he wants out of her. The Doughroaster's been trying to point out that she's ruining his dog but she's impervious to reason where Tash is concerned. She's convinced that The Doughroaster is far too hard on him. He's tried to tell her that Tash is a bit soft in the feet, but she doesn't buy it. Tash has also let The Doughroaster down badly in getting friendly with Lorna's cat. He even let it curl up against him on the porch in the sun the other day.

The next morning he hears the sound of a helicopter working along the top of the range. They're mustering Mangatane.

"My God!" says Lorna when she first sees all the unshorn

sheep The Doughroaster has in the woolshed. "Where did all these come from?"

"They look like Mangatane wethers to me," says The Doughroaster.

"How did they get here?" she says.

"I found them on the Boundary Creek faces on my way down yesterday. They must have come over the top to get out of that wind."

"We'll have to take them back, I suppose," she says.

"I don't think there's any hurry to do that," says The Doughroaster.

"What do you mean?"

"Well some of our sheep are over there among the Mangatane sheep and some of theirs are over here. We can just shear these and let them shear ours. They'll be easier to take back when they're shorn."

"Oh I see. How many do you think there are here?"

"Oh about two-fifty – three hundred," says The Doughliar.

"Then it should work out fair for both places," she says.

"Just about dead right," he agrees.

So while Johnny Knight's gang shear two hundred and fifty odd Bullock Creek sheep, The Doughroaster and the widow shear four hundred and sixty-seven Mangatane merinos and get nine bales of wool off them. It's hard work and takes them four days, by which time Lorna can see that The Doughroaster has underestimated the number of sheep they're handling.

"We've got more Mangatane sheep here than they've got of ours," she points out.

"Yeah I know," he says.

"Shouldn't we give them some of this wool?"

"No way," says The Doughroaster. "Some of our sheep have

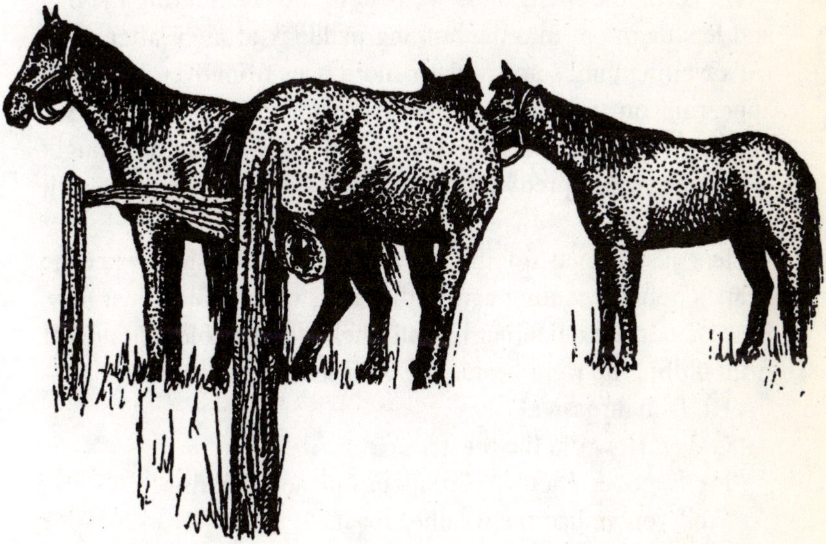

been on Mangatane for two or three years. They owe us wool if anything."

"Oh I see."

"Don't worry about it, Jake and I can sort it out."

"We must invite him and his wife over for a meal some time. I hardly know them."

"Sure," says The Doughroaster.

He keeps the Mangatane wethers in the shed during the day and lets them out into the holding paddock at night after dark. He's waiting until some of their shorn ones from over there start appearing on their high ridges. He can't use his dog just yet anyway. His feet must have been cut up worse than he thought because he's still pretty lame. He waits, he has to, and he's a bit uneasy.

He's just turned off the grinder in the woolshed when he hears a vehicle coming across the river, which is low just now. He gets outside quick but he can't head the Doubleburn ute off from pulling up right beside the woolshed. It's Tommy.

"Hi, Doughroaster."

"G'day. How did the muster go?"

"Pretty good. They've just about finished shearing."

"Well you've had the weather for it."

"Yeah, we were lucky this time."

"What are you doing over here?" says The Doughroaster.

"I'm on my way out to the pub to pick up the booze for the dance."

"What dance?"

"It's a hooley they put on in the Mangatane woolshed every year when the main shear's finished."

The Doughroaster's more concerned at the moment with what's being held in the Bullock Creek woolshed. They can plainly hear the stolen Mangatane wethers shuffling and bleating one thickness of corrugated-iron away from where Tommy's standing.

"What've you got in here?" he asks.

"Just a few half-fleece hoggets I'm crutching," says the Doughbluffer.

"Do you want a hand with them?" offers Tommy.

"Nar, she'll be right thanks Tommy. I've just about finished them. When's this dance supposed to be coming off?"

"Tomorrow night or the night after, starting at seven-thirty. I'll ring you and let you know as soon as I know for sure. Do you think you'll come?"

"Don't know. Depends." says The Doughroaster.

"Try and make it, Doughroaster. We had a great rage last year. Went on all next day. Don't forget to tell Mrs Fletcher it's on."

"Sure."

"I'll keep moving then. See you at the dance."

"Thanks for dropping in."

The Doughroaster leans on the gate for quite a while after Tommy's driven off.

That night there's still a bit of moon and The Doughroaster and his dog ease the Mangatane wethers up over the range, picking up about eighty Bullock Creek ones on the way, and they hunt the whole lot down the far side among the Mangatane flock. The dog's limping pretty badly again and The Doughroaster lets him sleep inside when they get back to the homestead. It's a relief to get those wethers safely off the place.

He's a bit late getting up for breakfast next morning, mainly because of having to carry the dog halfway home last night.

"You must be getting tired in your old age," jokes Lorna.

"Must be," he agrees, attacking a plateful of heated chops and fried potato.

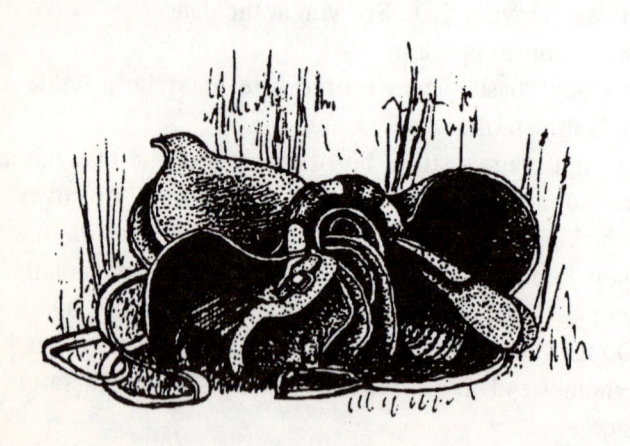

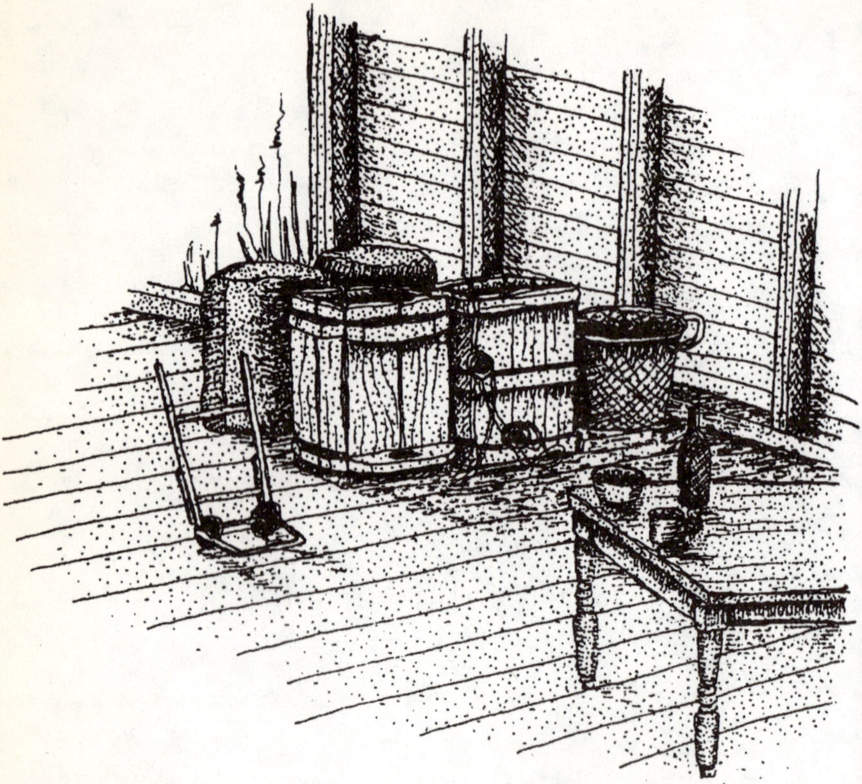

FOUR

A Merry Dance

The phone rings. Lorna answers it. It's Tommy. The woolshed dance is tomorrow night. The Doughroaster's completely forgotten to tell her about it. Lorna's keener on going to it than he is. She makes him dig out his good trousers and shirt and she washes and irons them.

When they're ready to leave for the dance The Doughroaster looks pretty good in his freshly-pressed grey trousers and white shirt and brown homespun pullover Lorna's just finished knitting for him. Lorna's wearing a dark blue dress, a black shawl and black high-heeled shoes. Her hair is hanging down wavy brown to her shoulders. It's the first time The Doughroaster's seen her done up like this and it makes him a bit nervous of her.

There's been a bit of rain overnight and the river's running high. They have to use the gelding to get across to the ute on the other side. He gets on and hauls her up behind him. She holds him round the waist, there's a whiff of some kind of perfume and a glimpse of one of her knees that causes The Doughroaster to lose concentration. He boots the gelding roughly out into the brown belly-deep rush of floodwater, fills one of his shoes with water and swears at the horse.

"Don't swear," says Lorna.

They stick the saddle and bridle in Lorna's waggon and he hobbles the horse and off they go in The Doughroaster's ute to the Mangatane woolshed dance. Lorna went to the one the year before last and seems quite excited about it. He's never heard her talk so much as on the way to this dance.

It's still daylight when they get to Mangatane, but the dance is already under way. Rows of cars and utes with sheep-crates strung with baling-twine; trail-bikes, muddy ones, lean against things here and there. Kids run around everywhere shouting. In the woolshed the women are gathered mainly around the food-trestles at one end and the men around the bar at the other, everyone talking at once. There must be a hundred people here. The music is a ghetto-blaster set up on a wool bale and operated by a group of boys and girls gathered around it, all wanting to play their favourite tapes. Three couples are dancing.

Lorna gets taken off among the ladies by Nancy Nathan. They're good mates, Lorna and Nancy. They ring each other up just about every day and they're always pleased to see each other. The Doughroaster sips from the bottle of beer he's been handed and waits out the conversation. He doesn't go these do's much. The Hog stops for a yarn and then drifts off to find someone or other. The Doughroaster leans there on the hydraulic woolpress and takes in the scene. Mostly strangers to him.

He notices a character they call The Culprit lurking around the edges of groups. The Culprit's the rouseabout on Mangatane and he's well-named. The Doughroaster heard quite a bit about him when he was on Doubleburn. Apparently The Culprit gets up to most of the mischief around the place. He'll swipe a bottle of wine from the homestead and then leave the empty bottle on the table in his hut. He'll swipe food from the store-room and leave the empty packets and cans lying around. If any of your gear goes missing, Ross Nathan reckons, it pays to check with The Culprit before you put in too much time looking for it. He'll wear someone's coat home and hang it up behind his door, or their boots and leave them on his porch. It's almost as though he's trying to get caught, and yet when he's confronted with the evidence he always denies knowing anything about it and swears that someone's got it in for him and planted the stuff on him.

Looking at The Culprit's ferretty manner and shifty eyes it's easy to believe he earns his reputation. The Doughroaster wonders why Johnny Knight keeps someone like The Culprit around – and then Johnny Knight and his wife arrive in a stir of noise and hand-shaking and back-slapping. Jake's dressed in western-style gear that actually glitters, topped off by a big white ten-gallon hat. He moves around being expansive, with his wife trailing along behind him. The Doughroaster watches the wife. She's a tall good-looking woman in a purple trouser-suit. She's acting as though she's surprised to see everyone she greets but she stops smiling too quick. This isn't her kind of country. They come near The Doughroaster. Jake strides forward, shoving out his hand.

"Howdy there, Doughroaster," he says, shaking hands too hard and too long. "How's things over on footrot flats?"

"We're getting by," says The Doughroaster, pulling his hand away.

Jake smiles harder and leans closer.

"Well make the most of it while you can, turkey. The winter's coming up. Then we'll see how you get by."

"I've seen more winters than you have, mate," says The Doughroaster.

"If the winter doesn't get you and the old girl off that place, the bank soon will. It couldn't pay its way, let alone pay off its debts."

"You farm your way, I'll farm mine," says The Doughroaster.

Jake raises his voice and laughs. "If you ever get the stock on that place sorted out let's know will you, Doughroaster. I'll have to come over and get a few photographs. It'll be a bloody miracle!" And he moves off and stops by the ghetto blaster and tells them to turn it off. The shed goes quiet and Jake begins what looks and sounds like his annual speech.

"When I first took over Mangatane, seven years ago now, I knew then that I was going to need the co-operation and friendship of my neighbours, pulling together, helping each other out when it's needed . . ."

The Doughroaster drifts outside. It's getting dark. They've turned on the outside light at the corner of the building. Most of the people have gone inside to listen to the speech, and there are only a few stragglers left out here drinking and talking. There's a saddled horse tied to the fence at the edge of the light from the shed. He saw some kids riding it around when they arrived.

He goes over and climbs the fence and strokes the horse's neck while he keeps an eye on who's coming and going There's a burst of laughter from inside the woolshed. He unhitches the reins and leads the horse along the fence away from the light and gets on it and rides it out into the paddock.

The stirrup-leathers are a bit short for him and he lets them out a couple of holes as he rides along, then he heads for the implement-shed, about a mile away out at the road. The Doughroaster's got a curiosity about that shed. The day he came to ask about the missing Bullock Creek sheep he noticed that Jake closed the door of the shed before he came over to talk to him. Jake doesn't want him to know what's in there.

He keeps well out from the woolshed road in case of anyone arriving or leaving. There's hardly any moon at all tonight, and some patchy cloud cuts out most of the starlight but his eyes adjust themselves to it and soon he can pick out enough to lift the horse into a canter in the easier places. Down the hill from the woolshed and off to find a gateway through into the next paddock and nearly gets caught in some headlights coming up the road.

It doesn't take all that long. He comes up behind the implement-shed and ties the horse to the steering-wheel of a wrecked tractor there, then he takes a look around the building. He has to be careful of noise because he can see the lights of the head-shepherd's house through some trees, less than a hundred yards up the road.

The front doors of the implement-shed are locked. The smaller back door's locked too, and the side window is jammed four inches open. He reaches in and feels around and one of the first things he touches is a screwdriver, a big one, lying on a workbench. There's some plastic containers and a chainsaw chain, a block of wood and an electric cord, which he pulls in and fishes up an electric drill, unplugged. He takes the screwdriver and goes round to the back door and feels for the hinges. Yes, he can get at them; they're on the outside.

He unscrews the hinges and lays the door against the wall of the building and slips inside. It's pitch black in here, he might as well be blind, and he hasn't even got a box of matches. This is starting to take too much time. He feels around the edge of the door and locates a light-switch, careful not to bump it on by accident, then he feels for the door lock and unsnibs it and shuts the door and puts two screws in each hinge and throws the other four out into the paddock. Then he goes inside and snibs the door onto lock again and feels for the light-switch.

He doesn't even know if the light's going to come on, and when it does the glare of it blinds him for a moment. Then, just for a second, or maybe two seconds, no more than three anyway, The Doughroaster sees what Johnny Knight doesn't want him to. Then off with the light, shut the door and grope blinded for the horse. Into the saddle and off across the paddock, cantering before he can see properly.

His eyes adjust. No car lights in sight. He might have got away with it. Then he makes a bad decision. Instead of risking going out near the road to get into the next paddock, he decides to cut straight across towards the woolshed lights and try and find a gate up that end of the fence.

The horse has given up trying to be lazy by this time and it's moving good under him. He converges with the fenceline and follows it for longer than he's happy about, looking for the gate that has to be along here somewhere. Suddenly he's ridden the horse up to its belly in a swamp. He drags its head round and heels it floundering and splashing back onto hard going again and follows the fence to back out near the road and nearly gets seen by headlights again getting through the gate, because the horse has got jumpy and he has to get off to open and close it.

He uses up more time looking for the next gate, which he must have fluked the first time. He can hear the music and see people walking round and standing in the light outside the woolshed, but now he's got another problem. The horse is blowing so hard that if he takes it any nearer someone's going to hear it so he gets off and leads it round until it settles down a bit.

He only meant to be gone for a few minutes but he's been away about an hour. Then he runs into another snag. When he leads the horse near the light to tie it to the fence where he got it from he has to quickly take it back into the dark before anyone sees it. It's plastered with mud and sweat and obviously just been ridden hard. He takes the saddle and bridle off it. It shakes itself and then lies down and starts rolling in the dust. Good, but it's taken more time. He hangs the saddle and bridle on the fence and climbs over into the light.

"Hey, Doughroaster!"

It's Tommy, with a bottle of beer in each hand.

"Where've you been?" he says. "I've been looking all over the place for you. Here, have a drink!"

The Doughroaster takes one of his bottles and drinks.

"Where've you been?" repeats Tommy. "Lorna's been looking for you and we couldn't find you anywhere."

"I've been around," says The Doughroaster. "You must have just missed me."

"Well you'd better go and find Lorna. She's inside last time I seen her."

The Doughroaster goes into the shed and stands behind a group at the edge of the dancing space. They're playing a loud modern song of some sort and the dance-floor's fairly crowded, some of them fox-trotting, some rock-and-rolling, some shuffling and some just standing on their own, jumping up and down in the same place. For a moment there The Doughroaster feels as out-of-date and old fashioned as a piece of blotting-paper. He doesn't see Lorna but suddenly she's right beside him.

"Where on earth have you been?" she says.

"Outside talking to some of the blokes," says The Doughfibber innocently.

"Well I must say you could at least have – My God! Look at you! What's happened to you?"

The Doughroaster looks down at himself. He's plastered with black mud, new pullover and all. That blasted swamp he rode into.

"I must have – er . . ." He's stuck for words right here.

She turns him round by the arm and pushes him in the back out the door and down the steps outside.

"What have you been *doing*?" she demands.

The Doughroaster's never seen her like this before, dressed up and going crook. She's like a stranger and it throws him out of gear.

"I came a gutser getting over the fence behind the shed there," he says.

"You're drunk!" she accuses him.

"Have had a few," he confesses.

"Well, I'm not going back in there with you like that."

"We might as well go home then," he says. "I've had enough of this place anyway."

"It's not even ten o'clock yet," she says. "I haven't even had a dance."

"I don't mind waiting out here if you want to stick around for a while," he tells her.

"Oh shut up!" she says, dragging him by the sleeve towards where the ute's parked.

"Don't swear," he says to cheer her up.

"Don't you talk to me like that, Barney Carter," she says. "I'm not your horse or your dog. You've ruined the whole dance."

The Doughroaster can't figure that out so he lets it drop.

"You still haven't explained what you've been doing," she says, slamming the ute door and reaching for the safety-belt. "How on earth did you get all that mud over your good clothes?"

"I was having a look round and got into a bit of a swamp in the dark," he tells her truthfully.

But she wouldn't have believed a lie either. She doesn't speak to him for the rest of the way home and just about all next day, which gives him time to think about what Johnny Knight didn't want him to see in the Mangatane implement shed. And next time they're in town he lets Lorna do most of their shopping while he takes care of some business of his own.

With the Bullock Creek sheep under control for the time being The Doughroaster turns his attention to the cattle. The first thing he has to do is fix up the cattleyards. They're so rotten and broken-down that he has to pull all the rails off one yard to patch the two others with. It's a mickey-mouse job but he's hoping he only has to use the yards once. They might hold together. There's supposed to be forty-four cows and heifers, sixteen steers and two bulls on Bullock Creek, but he can only find twenty-seven of the cows and seven steers and the two bulls. Most of the rest are on Mangatane.

The cattle are spooky; some of the yearlings have never been dogged or yarded before and none of the others are particularly keen to get yarded again. He finally gets them into the holding-paddock with the gelding steaming wet and hollow-flanked, and the dog flopping panting into every puddle and patch of shade he comes to. He's got them in the holding-paddock but they're pretty worked-up and he can't risk pushing them with the flimsy state the fences and yards are in, so he leaves them to settle down for a couple of hours. The younger bull's getting a bit nasty. He's charged the horse twice and the dog at every opportunity.

After lunch he rides out and moves the mob quietly along the fence and eases them into the yards. He gets the bulls and steers drafted off into the smaller yard and lets the cows back out onto the flats. He's got plans for those cows. They truck the two bulls and sixteen steers off to the sale in town.

"What are we going to do without bulls?" asks Lorna as they turn from watching the cattle-truck bounce and sway across the river. "I was quite fond of old Bully."

"I've got an arrangement with Mangatane to use their pedigree Angus bulls," says The Doughfibber.

"I hope it's not too expensive."

"Don't worry, they're doing it for us for free."

"Really! Isn't that nice of Johnny Knight. I used to think he was a bit of a meanie. It just goes to show you, doesn't it."

"Sure does," agrees The Doughroaster. "What have you decided about the horses?"

"I don't know. I suppose if they have to go they have to go."

"We don't need those horses, but we do need the grass they're eating. Most of them are brumbies anyway. We can't afford to keep them, it's as simple as that."

"Of course, you're right, we have to sell them."

So The Doughroaster rounds up the sixteen horses running on the Bullock Creek flats and trucks fourteen of them off to the same sale the bulls and steers have gone to, leaving three horses on the place: the Doubleburn gelding, Lorna's little black mare, Miranda, and a solid-looking little roan gelding he keeps back for a spare. Fourteen horses and eighteen head of cattle are good to get rid of off the place and he doesn't care much what they bring at the sale.

There's not much more he can do with the stock at this stage so The Doughroaster gets into a bit of essential maintenance on the place. He nails down the loose iron on the woolshed roof that's been annoying him, digs a drain to carry rainwater away from the sheepyards and does a bit of patchwork on them, and on the holding-paddock fence. Sitting out on the fenceline eating a mutton sandwich one day, The Doughroaster notices that his dog is putting on condition lately. In fact he's positively sleek. He hasn't had much work just lately, but that would hardly account for it.

He cuts down on the amount of meat he's been feeding him, but it doesn't seem to make any difference, Tash is getting *fat*.

Then one day, pulling a worn set of shoes off the Doubleburn gelding, he spots the dog trotting up towards the house looking furtive. The Doughroaster follows him and comes up the path just in time to see Lorna tipping half a bucketful of scraps onto some newspaper by the back steps for him. The dog and the widow both look guilty when they see him coming up the path.

"What the hell do you want to go feeding-up my bloody dog like that for?" he says. "Do you realise what happens if he can't work?"

"Don't you go swearing at me, Barney Carter," she says. "He's hungry, the poor thing, look at him."

Tash has taken advantage of the distraction and is getting stuck into the heap of scraps.

"He's a dog," says The Doughroaster. "He'll eat anything you give him."

"Go on with you!" she says hotly. "You'd work and starve the poor thing to death."

"You're *feeding* him to death."

"Rubbish," she says, and she stoops down and takes Tash's

head in her arms. Tash condescends to stop eating long enough to rub his face on her.

The Doughroaster knows when he's beaten.

"Okay, you feed the bloody dog then,' he says, and he goes back to shoeing the horse.

He gives up feeding the dog altogether, and the dog stays disgustingly fat. He can't even keep Tash on the chain because whenever Lorna sees him tied up she comes and lets him go, like some kind of pet lap-dog. He's only using the dog these days to keep the wethers high and the ewes on the lower faces, but he doesn't like him being too heavy on his feet on this stony country, doesn't like it at all, but there's nothing he can do about it without upsetting Lorna Fletcher and he doesn't like doing that either. A man just has to accept some things.

Lorna sits at the kitchen table doing the station accounts.

"We've got five thousand one hundred and twenty dollars for the bulls and steers, and fifteen hundred and eighty dollars for the horses. That's six thousand seven hundred dollars!"

"Good," grunts The Doughroaster from behind his magazine. "We need money more than we need cattle and horses on this place. And we're still overstocked to hell with sheep."

"Can't we sell some of them?"

"It'd cost us more to truck them to the sale than we'd get for them. It'd be the same as paying someone to take them away."

"What can we do then?" she asks.

"Don't worry about it," he says. "I'll think of something."

And so The Doughroaster works on through the summer, keeping himself busy patching and repairing the broken-down buildings and fences and gear on Bullock Creek station and giving them a hand on Doubleburn whenever they need it, and keeping his mind off why he's really here.

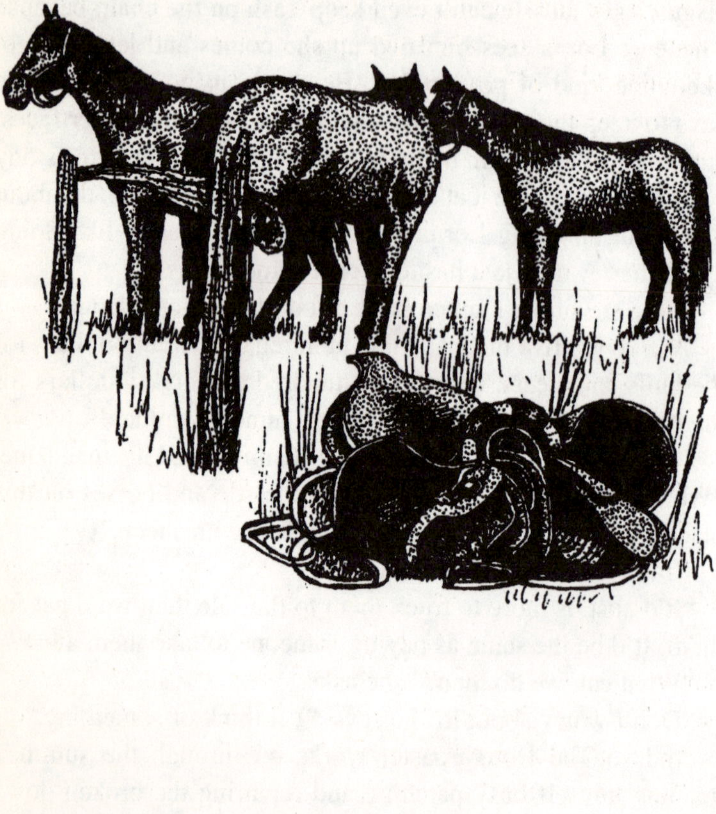

FIVE

OVER THE TOP

It's been raining steadily for two days and nights and they're cut off from the road again. The Doughroaster and Lorna are just finishing breakfast when the phone rings. It's Nancy on Doubleburn. The Doughroaster catches bits of the conversation.

"What was all that about?" he asks Lorna when she comes back.

"That was Nancy. They've got Alan and The Culprit over there."

"What are they doing there?"

"They couldn't get back to Mangatane last night. Their road's slipped away."

"So Mangatane's cut off?"

"Yes. Nancy says Ross is worried they might try and use the road from the Mangatane end. It's dangerous."

"Yeah? I think I'll give Ross a ring and find out what's going on."

He gets Ross on the phone. "What's the story with the Mangatane Road, Ross?"

"The whole hillside's gone at Boulder Bluffs, about a hundred yards of it. And it's taken the phone-wires out. I've just had a call from the County Engineer. It's going to take them a week or more to open it up again."

"So they're cut off over there?"

"Yeah, and we're a bit worried about them. They reckon there's a sheer five-hundred-foot drop into the river at the Mangatane end, right on the hairpin bend at the start of the bluffs."

"Hell. I don't like the sound of that. Is there any way we can let them know?"

"No. That's the trouble. They've got a chopper standing by, but it could be days before they can get off the ground, with all this low cloud. And if they try to use that road – I don't like to think about it."

"Nor me," says The Doughroaster. "I'd better ride over there and see if I can head them off."

"You couldn't even get out over the river there just now, could you?" says Ross.

"No, I'll cut over the top."

"You can't get over there. You'll kill yourself!"

"Ah – I've got a bit of track I've found. I reckon I can make it all right."

"I don't like it, Doughroaster, but if you think you can make it you're the only one who could possibly get through to them."

"I'll get goin'," says The Doughroaster.

He puts on his jersey, coat, hat and boots, tells Lorna there's nothing to worry about, calls up the dog, saddles the gelding and lifts it into a canter across the holding-paddock to warm it up, and then boots it up the track to the top of the range. He has to stop and fix a washed-out part of the track and it takes him about two hours to make it to the top. He gets off to lead the horse along into the saddle and, blast it, it's thrown a front shoe. He knows the hoof will chip away on the rock and be hard to keep a shoe on for a while after this, but he has to keep going now.

The wind, only blustery in the valley, is really roaring up here. Misty wet cloud streams past him, dripping off his face. He has to turn his back on the heavier gusts and hang onto his horse, its whipping mane stinging his face. The dog lies flat and hooks his claws into the rock. He picks his way through onto Mangatane. He's never had a horse down this side of the range before, but by turning back and trying another place when he gets blocked and taking a couple of risks he makes it out onto open tussock.

It's still very steep but he can make better progress now, and he starts to remember what he's doing this for and pushes the horse a bit faster. He catches glimpses of the greener flats down through the blowing misty rain, but now there's a fence cutting right across the ridge he's travelling down. He doesn't hesitate. Gets the fencing-pliers out of his saddle-sack and cuts the fence and carries on. He's over the worst of it.

It must be getting on for midday when he gets down to the station. He tries the head-shepherd's house first. No one home. He canters the half-mile up to the homestead. No fresh tyre-marks on the road, but that could mean anything in this rain, which is getting heavier. He ties the gelding to the fence and hears voices inside as he goes round the house to the door and knocks. Jake's wife opens it and gets a surprise to see him.

"Doughroaster! What on earth are you doing here?"

"Got a message for you," he says taking off his coat.

Jake appears in the doorway behind her. "What's going on, Doughroaster? You'd better come in."

Alan's wife is here. They sit at the table in the big kitchen. The Doughroaster's never been in here before.

"Cup of tea?" says Jake's wife.

"Thanks," says The Doughroaster. "Has anyone tried to use the road out of here today?"

"No," says Jake. "There must be a slip. Alan and The Culprit didn't get home last night. Our phone's out, too. We were just going to drive out to see what's going on."

"Alan and The Culprit are okay. They spent the night at Doubleburn. Your road's gone at Boulder Bluffs, about a hundred yards of it, they reckon."

"Then we *are* cut off," says Jake's wife, pouring The Doughroaster a weak cup of tea in a china cup.

"Yeah. Ross says it's going to take them a week to open up the road again."

"Hell," says Jake. "I've got to get into town tomorrow. It's important. And I can't call up a chopper, even if they could fly in this. How bad is the road, Doughroaster?"

"Haven't seen it myself," says The Doughroaster.

"How did you get here if you didn't come round the road?" says Jake's wife.

"I rode over."

"Rode over where?" says Jake.

"From Bullock Creek. Over the top."

"You rode a horse over the top of the Barker?" says Jake.

"Yeah."

"Like hell you did!"

The Doughroaster drinks from his cup and puts it down and says, "Look Jake, I rode over here to warn you not to use your road because I was the only one who could get to you. The road's dangerous, don't go near it. They reckon there's a straight drop into the river on that sharp bend at this end of the bluffs. And if you think I came over here to tell you that for a joke you want to try it yourself some time."

"Sorry, Doughroaster," says Jake. "I never heard of anyone getting a horse across there, that's all. I didn't know it was possible. Thanks."

"Yes, thanks, Doughroaster," says Jake's wife. "Can I get you something to eat?"

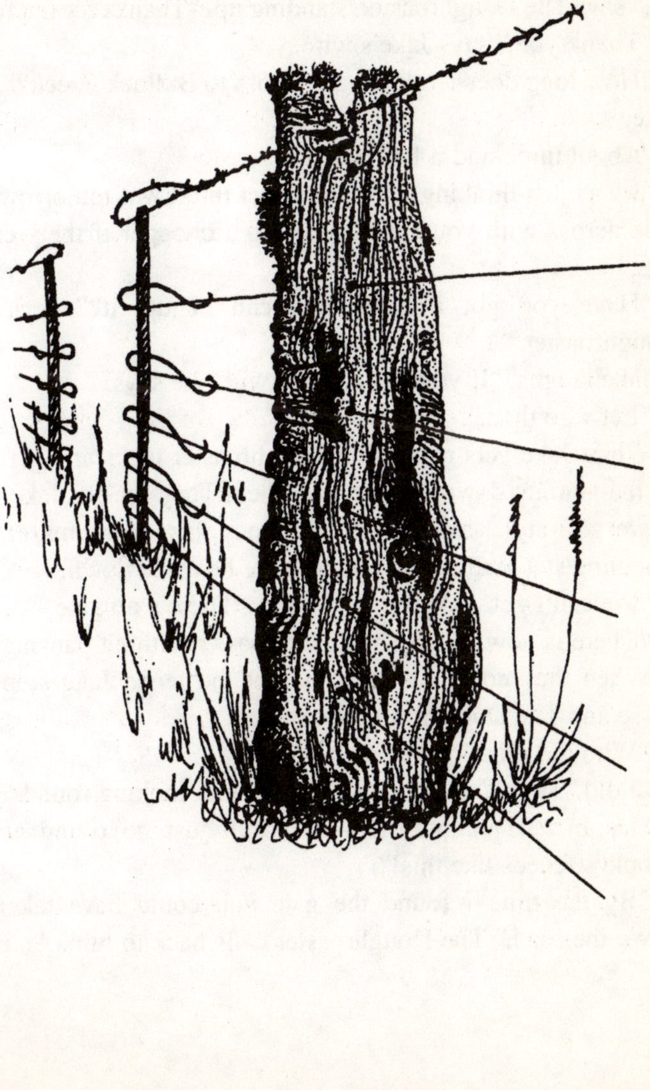

"Yeah," he says. "And a dry pair of strides wouldn't go astray either."

Jake's clothes are too big for him, but they're dry and warm. They all eat lunch.

"Well I'll get back to Bullock Creek while the rain's eased off," says The Doughroaster, standing up. "Thanks for the feed."

"Thank you," says Jake's wife.

"How long does it take to get across to Bullock Creek?" says Jake.

"About three-and-a-half hours."

"I was just thinking. I've got to get into town tomorrow. If I rode across with you I could call up a chopper if the weather lifts."

"Have you got a horse that can handle it?" says The Doughroaster.

Jake laughs, "If yours can, mine will," he says.

"Let's go then."

While Jake gets ready The Doughroaster tacks another shoe on the gelding down at their woolshed. They set off. Jake rides a western-style saddle on a prancy big grey mare. The Doughroaster leads them up the ridge he came down.

"We can't get up here," says Jake. "There's no gate."

"There is now," says The Doughroaster without pausing.

When they come to where he cut the fence Jake stops his horse and The Doughroaster doesn't.

"Who did this?" calls out Jake.

"I did," says The Doughroaster without looking round.

"Damn it, Doughroaster. You can't just go round cutting people's fences like this!"

"By the time I found the gate you could have taken off down the road," The Doughroaster calls back to him. And Jake has to boot his horse to catch up.

"We're not riding up *there*," says Jake as they approach a steep gut running fifty yards up through a cleft in the rock.

"I am," says The Doughroaster, booting the gelding lunging and scrambling up the rocky gully and out onto a little tussock bench. Looking back he watches Jake's horse only just make it. Jake's breathing as hard as if he'd carried the horse.

"Bloody hell, Doughroaster," he gasps. "You'll get us killed!"

"I'll get us to Bullock Creek if that brumby of yours can stay on its feet," says The Doughroaster. "This bit up ahead's a bit tricky. We'll probaby have to lead 'em up it."

Jake looks up at the steep crumble of broken rock ahead of them and stops.

"I'm not taking this horse up there, mate. It's not used to this sort of stuff. It's a valuable animal."

The Doughroaster turns his horse to look back at him.

"Leave it here, then."

Jake looks back down to the flats and then up at the windstrewn clouded peaks. He gets off his horse and leads it up to where The Doughroaster stands. The wind flattens the brim of Jake's big hat against his head.

"Can't we walk from here?" he says.

"You can if you like. I'm taking my horse."

Jake's horse makes the decision for them. It refuses to tackle the rock slope. The Doughroaster brings his horse back down and they put Jake's saddle on the gelding and tie the bridle and The Doughroaster's saddle on top of it and let Jake's horse go. Then they pick their way up the side of the mountain.

The wind and cloud seem to have got a bit worse since The Doughroaster came across here earlier. He can only see a few yards in this. The gelding lunges up onto a sloping shelf behind him and a sudden blast of wind makes him hang onto the rock with both hands until it passes and subsides into an ordinary gale.

He looks for Jake and sees him lying against the rockface below him. Jake crawls up and The Doughroaster hauls him up onto the shelf beside him.

"We can't go on in this," shouts Jake. "We'll have to go back."

"The top's just over there," shouts back The Doughroaster. "It's not so bad on the other side."

"We'll never make it. We can't even see where we're going!"

"The dog knows the way. We only have to follow him."

Another roar of wind flattens them against the rock.

"You're crazy!" shouts Jake. "We've got to get out of this. We're going to get blown off the mountain! I'm going back."

The Doughroaster doesn't reply. There's a lull in the wind. He leads the horse off behind Tash towards the saddle in the top of the range. Jake's too scared not to follow. They scramble out onto the top of the ridge and then The Doughroaster gets scared. The cloud's so thick he has to rely on his dog and his memory to find the way over towards where the track goes down to Bullock Creek. The wind's fairly shrieking up here. The gelding gives a start as Jake's big hat flicks past and vanishes in the streaming cloud. The Doughroaster stands hanging onto the horse and sees his dog blown, rolling, across the stony slope and out of sight over a ridge of broken rock. Jake slams into him and he has to grab him to stop him getting blown past towards the edge. They cling to the horse and wait for the wind to take a breather so they can move.

There's a bit of stone stinging in the wind and the gelding's getting panicky. If it bolts up here it'll go over the edge and kill itself, but all The Doughroaster can do about it is hold the horse as tight as he can and wait for a break in the wind. It's a long couple of minutes. The wind momentarily eases and they move off, and they just get over the brow towards Bullock Creek when another tumult whips around them and pins them clinging to the rocks.

They have to watch for broken gusts of wind on this side, buffeting suddenly from any direction. One of those hitting you when you're trying to negotiate one of the tricky parts of the track and you wouldn't stand a chance of staying on the ridge. As they begin to pick their way down the ridge Tash limps up out of the mist with a patch of hair bruised off his shoulder. The Doughroaster had forgotten about him but he's pleased to see him.

An hour later they reach the bottom of the ridge and take a breather. Jake flops onto the ground. He's completely exhausted and still looks a bit wild-eyed from the fright he's had. The Doughroaster lets him rest for a few minutes and then leads the way towards the holding-paddock, with Jake stumbling along behind.

"You're bloody mad, Doughroaster," gasps Jake. "You can't go riding horses around in places like that. You'll kill yourself!"

"Haven't yet," says The Doughroaster.

"You could easy have got us killed up there, you bloody lunatic!"

The Doughroaster ignores him and they get to the shed and he lets the gelding go and they go up to the house. Lorna's glad to see them safe. She makes tea and mutton sandwiches while they get into dry clothes. Jake eats and falls asleep on the sofa. Lorna rings Doubleburn to let them know they're okay on Mangatane while The Doughroaster gets the fire stoked up to dry things out.

Next morning the cloud-ceiling has lifted to halfway up the range. A chopper lands in drizzle by the old Bullock Creek woolshed and lifts Jake away to his urgent business in town.

"He's a quiet chap, isn't he," says Lorna as they turn from watching the chopper disappear.

"He can be sometimes," agrees The Doughroaster.

He hasn't got any more to say about their trip across the range than Jake has at the moment.

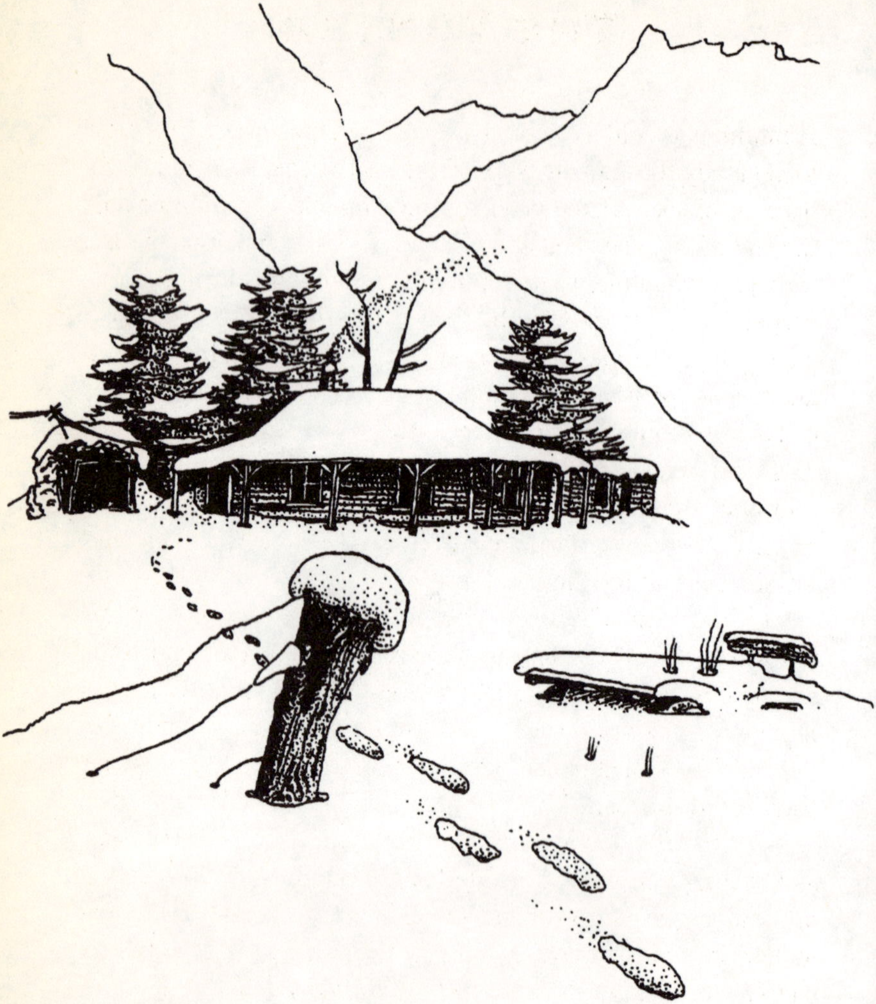

SIX

The Winter

A morning as cold as a crowbar tells The Doughroaster it's time to get ready for the winter. He sharpens the chainsaw and cuts a heap of blocks off the dead macrocarpa that's leaning against the end of the woolshed and fills the woodshed up at the house. Last year when the water-supply to the homestead froze Lorna carried her water up from the river in plastic buckets. The usual water-supply comes from a spring up the hill through an alkathene pipe lying along the top of the ground, probably one of the first things on the place to freeze up. So he gets on the roof and fixes up some of the sagging spouting and gets rainwater running into the tank for the first time in years. He butchers five big Mangatane wethers he's been saving and Lorna packs all the meat in the freezer.

They work out a list of supplies for when they get snowed and flooded in. They're going to need sacks of potatoes and flour and onions; butter, yeast, sugar, tea and canned food; socks and longjohns, candles in case of power-cuts and a spare handle for the axe. The Doughroaster wants a new pair of boots and some leggings for himself; Lorna wants warm gloves and a skijacket.

They go off to town in the ute with a bale of wool on the back and exchange it for a whole ute-load of supplies. Lorna wears a dress today, a grey one, but the first time The Doughroaster notices it is when they've done all their shopping and they're halfway through lunch in the *DeLuxe Restaurant and Tearooms*.

"What happened to your overalls today?" he jokes.

But she doesn't seem to get the joke.

And The Doughroaster and the widow drive home to Bullock Creek in silence with their load of supplies for the winter.

There's only an hour of sun each day at the homestead now before it gets cut off by the deep narrowness of the Bullock Creek valley; there's a steely chill in the air. The Doughroaster knows it isn't going to be easy to get two-and-a-half thousand sheep through the winter on this place unless it's a real mild season, and buying in hay or any other kind of feed is out of the question. Not promising, but he's got a trick or two up his sleeve yet.

The sun goes from the valley floor altogether and the valley freezes. Hobnails clump onto mud frozen as hard as wood. Then blue-grey banks of cloud settle around the peaks of the Barker Range and The Doughroaster and his dog get up there quick and muster everything they can find down out of it. He manages to collect about five hundred of the wethers and push them over onto Mangatane and round onto their winter block among their flock. The rest he hunts down into the valley on the Bullock Creek side, just ahead of the snow. That night the tops get covered in two feet of snow and they'll probably stay covered for the next five months or so.

He decides to muster what sheep he can get down out of Bullock Creek Valley and bring them out into the open, where they'll have more chance of surviving. Up Bullock Creek he finds that every seepage has turned into a thick sheet of ice.

Every trickle has become a stalagmite or whichever, some of them up to twelve feet long and three feet thick. The swampy places are frozen solid and the ground itself is so iced-up that it's tricky to walk on any slope. The fog meets the rock and freezes, building up fantastic patterns, but The Doughroaster sees no beauty in it. He ties the gelding to a matagouri bush and carries on up the valley on foot.

He musters a few bunches of sheep but he has to leave some of them behind in the finish. He puts the dog out to head a bunch of mixed ewes and wethers on a high shelf, but before Tash can get there he starts sliding down the icy slope towards a three-hundred-foot bluff. He manages to stop himself a few yards short of the bluff and The Doughroaster whistles him round and down out of it and leaves the sheep to try and survive up there. Some of them probably will. He comes out of there with forty-four sheep and hunts them up the flats among the main mob. Not a bad day's work.

They draft out the mob, eleven hundred ewes and nine hundred wethers; the ewes go up the flats and the wethers go down the flats. He keeps them on the lower slopes until it snows again and gives him a snow-boundary to keep them down. It snows again and sleets and rains and freezes. The Doughroaster gives in and shifts into the spare bedroom inside the house. Too cold out there in his glass-walled sunporch. And Tash shifts onto a sack on the porch and waits for Lorna to open the door a crack and smuggle him in by the fire when they think The Doughroaster's not looking.

There's a break in the weather; it's only raining, The grader's been up the road and cleared the snow and Lorna decides to take some hanks of spun wool into the craft-shop and pick up one or two things they need. The Doughroaster rides her across the river on the gelding and as soon as she's gone he canters off and rounds up all the cows, twenty-seven of them, and pushes them across the river and out onto the road. He's been waiting for a chance to do this.

It's raining steady and hard as he heads them with the dog and turns the mob up the Mangatane Road. He gets past them and rides along in front, letting Tash bring them up behind him. If anyone comes up the road he's only got to turn his horse round and he's heading back to Bullock Creek with this mob of strays he's just caught up with.

He gets them through to the Mangatane boundary, about a mile and a half short of the homestead, without being seen, but this is the tricky bit. It's still raining and the wind's got up and blowing curtains of sleet across the tussocked hillsides. He ties the gelding in a gully out of sight of the road and gets the wire-strainers out of his split-sack, and while Tash holds the cattle there he undoes the fence at the strainer and folds the first span back out of the way and hunts them through and up onto the tussock face.

By letting go a tie-down just along the fence he manages to get the fence wires done up in the same twists they were in before. He loses a bit of tension on the tie-down but no one's going to notice that. Then he shoves the cattle up the ridge and over the other side, where he knows the Mangatane herd is scattered through the brush and tussock on their rough block.

As he gets back near the road it's just dark enough for a car coming up the road to have to have its lights on, heading towards Mangatane. The Doughroaster drops into the tussock and holds his dog down while it goes past. It's The Culprit, weaving his way back from the pub.

"That could have been a bit embarrassing about an hour ago:" he mutters to himself as he gets back over the fence onto the road.

He gets on his horse. Tash is getting a bit footsore and bony by this time so The Doughroaster calls him over and hoists him by the scruff onto the saddle in front of him, and Tash rides all the way back to Bullock Creek on the knee pads of The

Doughroaster's saddle in the rain. The river's up and rising when they get there. Lorna's not back yet. The Doughschemer likes this one. The rain's washed out all his marks and he's made it back to Bullock Creek without being seen by anyone at all.

Lorna arrives back only an hour after him, but by this time the river's running too high for the horse, and she has to drive on to Doubleburn and stay with the Nathans. The Doughroaster has the place to himself for four days, waiting for the river to go down. He can tell on the phone that Lorna's enjoying the break on Doubleburn.

He hasn't realised how much cleaning-up Lorna must do all the time to keep the house getting in the mess he has it in. The river's going down, Lorna should be able to get across by morning, so he spends a couple of hours tidying up the kitchen, but there's still food and paper and dishes and cups on the table and sink bench and mantelpiece and floor when she arrives home. She cleans it up while he makes them a cup of tea. She's in a good humour today and teases him about Doughroasters who leave the camp in a mess.

But this Doughroaster's got more than dirty dishes on his mind just now. Mangatane is wintering seven hundred and fifty sheep for him, and all the cattle, until they get sprung, and that's quite a big help, but he still has more than two thousand sheep to keep fed and he doesn't like the way this winter is getting stuck into them so early. Already his available grazing area has shrunk by two-thirds, and even if what's left was *good* grazing it wouldn't be anywhere near enough.

They've been sitting out three days of storms in front of the open fire in the homestead kitchen. Lorna spins wool. The Doughroaster reads *National Geographic* about vast dry hot deserts and forgets about the freezing sodden

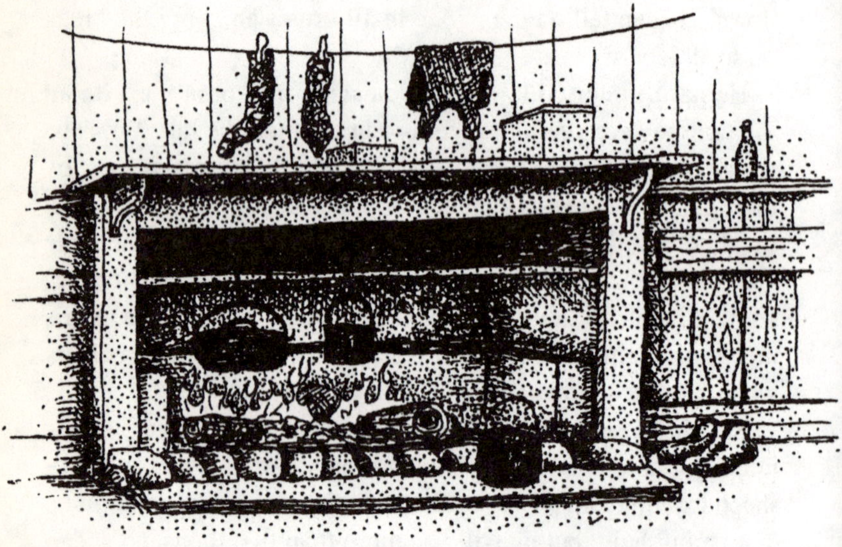

turbulent world outside.

Lorna answers the phone. It's Nancy Nathan, he can tell. They talk for quite a while and when Lorna comes back she says, "They've started feeding-out to the ewes on Doubleburn."

"Hay?"

"Yes. Ross thinks we might be in for a hard winter."

"He's right so far," says The Doughroaster.

Lorna takes up her spinning, he raises his magazine.

"Barney?" she says.

"What?"

"Where do you come from?"

"How do you mean?" he says, lowering his book.

"Well, where's your home?" she says.

"I've got a place up north, but I spent most of my time on high-country places like this when I was a young bloke. Something like this, anyway," he adds.

"Why did you move up north?"

The Doughroaster looks through the gap in the curtains at the whirling rain and sleet.

"The winters," he says. "I'd done pretty good on a leasehold block I had over Hawera way, and I sold it and bought three hundred and eighty acres of scrub and bush in Taranaki and broke it in. Been farming it ever since, about twenty years. Sheep and cattle mainly."

"Are you married?" she asks.

"I was for a while there," he says.

"Do you have any children?"

"Yeah, three of them."

"Boys?"

"Two of 'em are. The two oldest."

She gets it out of him. How he met his wife when he was still breaking in his farm. How they married and had two sons, Derek and then Chris, and quite a bit later a daughter called Susie. How his wife suddenly up and left him and the kids, and divorced him three years later to marry a baker in Nelson. How the boys started coming home from college telling him he was too old-fashioned for today's farming; how they had to modernise and diversify if they were to survive; venison, goat-fibre, cropping, embryo-transplants, everything computerised. How he couldn't understand it all and they'd always end up arguing.

And he tells her how he got them together when Susie was home from boarding-school and made the deal with them – he leaves the boys to run the farm for a year. If they prove they can do it they can take half the farm each and lease Susie's share off her until she decides what she wants to do with it. All Barney wants to keep for himself is the forty-acre block between the bush and the river on the far side. And Derek and Chris and Susie all agreed to the deal.

"No interfering?" he remembers Chris saying.

"Guarantee it," he'd promised.

"So I took off to have a look around me old stamping ground and left them to it. And here I am," he concludes.

"Have you been in touch with them since you left?" Lorna asks.

"No."

"How long have you been away?"

"I left in October, about seven months ago."

"They must be worried about you. Don't you miss them?"

"Not a hell of a lot."

"I think you should at least ring them and let them know you're all right," she says.

"I promised not to interfere."

"That's not interfering. They'll be worried about you."

"Nar. Don't like phones much anyway. It'd only look like I was checking up on them."

"Nonsense. You get on that phone and let your family know where you are and what you're doing."

He argues the toss a bit more but she wins, and The Doughroaster gets through on the phone in the hallway and suddenly he hears Derek's voice, "Carters' place."

"G'day," says The Doughroaster.

"Dad! Is that you – Chris, it's Dad! – Where are you? We've been worried about you."

"I'm working on a place down south."

"Are you okay?"

"Yeah. Everything all right up there?"

"Sure, Dad. When are you coming home?"

"Don't know. I've got a bit to do down here yet. Is Susie okay?"

"Yes. She just went back to school the day before yesterday. She's all right, but she misses you Dad."

"Tell her I miss her too."

"Sure, Dad. When do you think . . ."

The phone is snatched away from Derek and Chris comes on. Chris, the cheeky one.

"Dad! Hi! When are you coming home?"

"G'day."

"Are you all right? Where are you?"

"I'm working on a station in Otago."

"When are you coming home?"

"When I've finished what I'm doing down here. How's the farm going?"

"Real good, Dad. We've got so much to show you. You won't know the place!"

"Save it for when I get back. What's the weather like up there?"

"Lousy. It's been raining for the past two days."

"It's not the best here either just now. Well I'd better get off this phone . . ."

"Hang on Dad. What's your address and phone number there?"

He gives them to him and says goodbye a few more times and hangs up. His family and the farm up north seem as remote from him as something he read about once. He's living a different kind of life in a different place, even his name is different. The Doughroaster feels a touch of sadness.

"Get through all right?" Lorna asks when he comes back into the kitchen.

"Yeah, quicker than getting through to Doubleburn."

"Have they been missing you?"

"Looks like they might have a bit," he admits. "They're getting on okay though. They know how to look after themselves, they're used to it."

"Do you ever miss being married?" she asks him.

"Did a bit at first."

"Don't you believe in it any more?"

"What, marriage?"

"Yes."

"I'm not that stupid."

"How do you mean?"

"Just try bringing up three kids on your own and running a farm as well and you'll soon see what I mean. It's a job that needs both to do it properly. Men and women are different. There's some things that's better done by a woman, and there's some things that's better done by a man, and there's some things that's better done by both. And there's some things that's better left alone altogether," he adds.

"What's that again?" she says.

But The Doughroaster's getting the uncomfortable feeling that he's said too much already today.

"Ar – nothin'."

"Would you like a cup of tea?" she says.

"Sure, if you're making one."

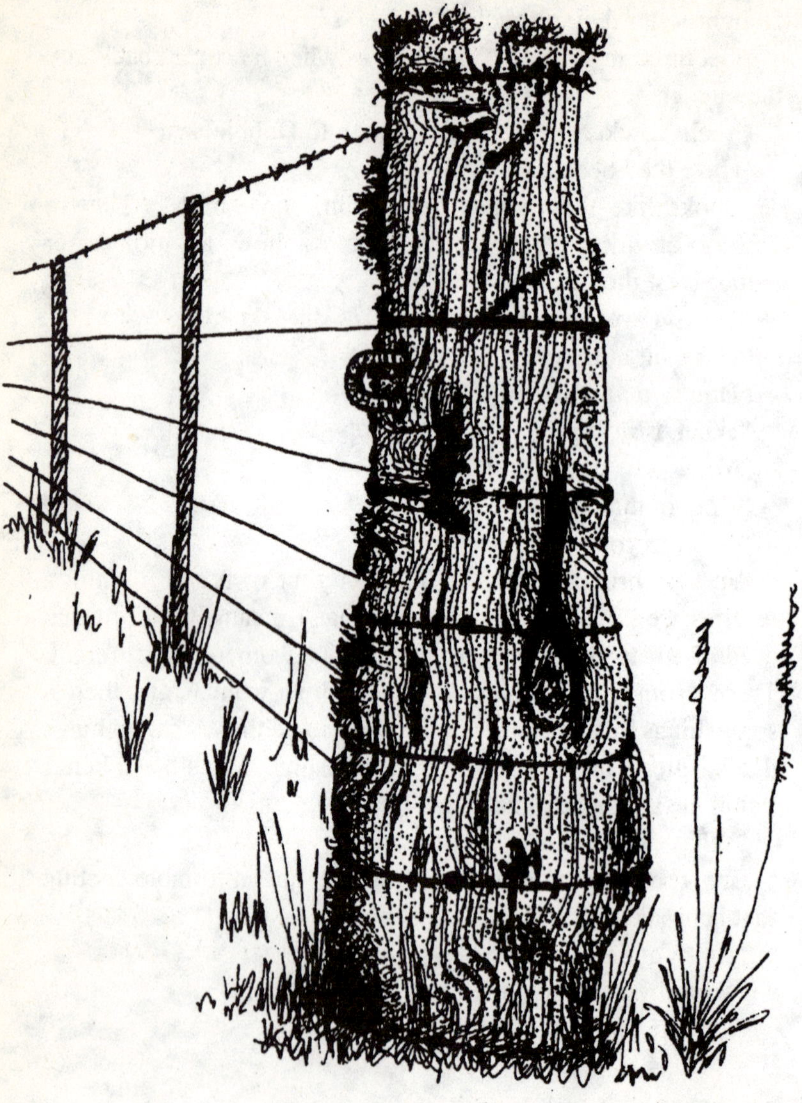

SEVEN

THE HOLDING-PADDOCK GATEPOST

Day after day, whenever the weather lets him, The Doughroaster rides the low-country, dragging weak sheep out of snowdrifts and keeping the mobs on the safer ground. And the weather doesn't let up on him, as front after front hits the Barker Range and lashes it with storms. All he can do is keep going and hope for a break in the weather and an early spring.

He comes in from the sheep and Lorna's talking to Derek on the phone. She hands it to him.

"G'day," he says.

"We've been wondering if you need any help down there," says Derek.

"No, we're okay."

"Well if you need a hand one of us can get away any time."

"Thanks, but we're managing so far."

"I don't know, Dad, two people running a twenty thousand acre property. You must be run off your feet."

"Its not that bad. It's a different kind of farming to what you're used to."

"It must be. Well let's know if you need anything. We've got this place pretty well under control at the moment," says Derek.

"That's good to hear. If we need any help we'll let you know. Are Chris and Susie okay?"

"Yes, they're fine. Lorna sounds nice."

"She's okay. I've just come in off the hill, I'd better go and get some of this wet gear off."

Ross Nathan rings The Doughroaster to tell him that a chopper heading for Doubleburn has spotted a bunch of sheep snowbound on a terrace above the Bullock Creek flats. He doesn't often need help with the stock but this day he gets Lorna to ride out with him to snow-rake the trapped sheep down onto the flats. They tie their horses at the foot of the slope and claw their way for several hundred feet up through the snow to the terrace, where fourteen of the wethers are huddled in a bunch, surrounded by a thick wall of snow. They've started to eat the wool off one another.

The Doughroaster breaks through to them and gets Lorna to lead the way down to the flats, treading a passage through the snow, while he and the dog keep them moving from behind. It's been snowing on and off and as they make their way down the slope a sudden change in the feel of the weather makes The Doughroaster stop and look round. It's getting darker than it ought to be. He can't see the flats down there any more and a thick flurry of snow almost blots out Lorna from his view. It closes in as he watches and begins to snow thickly. He shoves a slow sheep with his foot and calls out to Lorna, his voice distorted and muffled by the snow, "How far are you from the bottom?"

"I can't see it," she calls back, "but it mustn't be far now."

"Hurry it up, will you," he shouts down to her. "I don't like the look of this weather."

She's only fifty yards ahead of him, with the sheep strung out in single-file behind her, but The Doughroaster can now only see the nearest six or eight sheep. The weak wether collapses again and he can't get it to stay on its feet this time. He looks after Tash and the last sheep disappearing in the whirling snow and gets out his knife and cuts the wether's throat and hurries to catch up with the others.

They make it down onto the flats and leave the wethers with another small mob that's there, then they flounder off through the fresh snow to get the horses. And they're lucky to find them, two dark smudges glimpsed briefly through the curtains of snow as they're about to fumble past them. It's a mile and a half back to the homestead and The Doughroaster knows that if Lorna's as cold as he is they need to get there pretty soon.

"Let's keep moving," he says as he helps her onto her horse. "I don't like the look of this."

He mounts the gelding, "Keep me in sight whatever you do," and they move off through the snow. It's deep here and the horses are soon getting tired from plunging from snowdrift to snowdrift. The snow seems to be being made on the spot and growing on everything. They've been going for maybe twenty minutes when The Doughroaster sees something that makes him stop and dismount. Lorna rides up to him, "What's wrong?" she says.

"These are our tracks," he tells her, indicating the almost covered row of dents in the snow. "And we only made them a little while ago."

"What does that mean?"

"It means we're wandering in circles."

"We're lost!"

"That's right. We're somewhere out on the flats between the station and Boundary Creek, and if we don't get in out of this soon we're going to be in serious trouble."

"What can we do?"

"The dog might know where home is from here, but getting him to show us . . ."

"We have to try it," she says.

"Okay, we'll give it a go, but we'd better lead these horses for a while. They're getting pretty weak on it. Keep my horse in front of you and if you lose sight of him yell out."

He whistles Tash who comes jumping through the snow.

"Waleggo, Tash. Get in behind!"

And of course Tash goes in front like he always does when he's told to get in behind. He jumps off through the snow in a direction that worries The Doughroaster. There's a thirty foot drop into the river over there somewhere and in these conditions you'd be over the edge before you knew it, but Tash seems to know what he's doing so they follow.

They're completely whited-out now, visibility is barely the length of a horse. He has to keep telling the dog to get moving because he's getting tired from the effort needed to break a trail through more than two feet of fresh powdery snow, especially on this surface. This whole area is a series of heaps and hollows left by the old gold-miners and The Doughroaster knows that they can't travel much further on the energy they and the horses have left. The snow has flattened everything out, and they can only sprawl and flounder from one powdery hollow and into the next, getting tangled and tripped by the matagouri and briar hidden in the snow.

He drops up to his pockets into a deep drift, and suddenly the gelding lands on top of him and grinds him deeper into the snow in its efforts to get back onto its feet. He's fighting for breath and as the weight goes off him he gets a tooth-jarring bang on the thigh from a hoof. He gets his head out of the snow and gasps in a few breaths of air. The horse is standing there and he hauls himself up and stands hanging onto the saddle, trying to get his breath back. Lorna and her mare have gone into the same ditch a few yards along but he can barely see them, vague

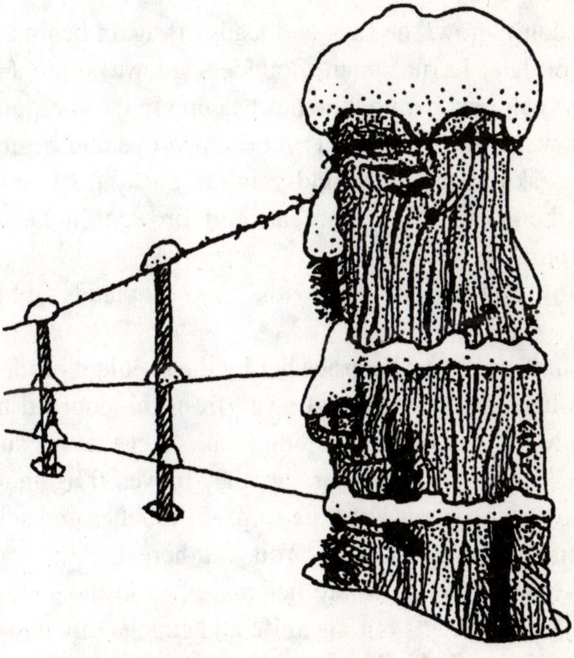

shapes fumbling to their feet in the whiteness.

They flounder on for a while, no telling time now, and then Lorna's horse goes down with a thud and lies on its side in the snow without trying to get up again, and already it begins to get covered. The Doughroaster wades back and drags its head up and bullies it onto its feet.

"We can't afford to give her a rest," he says. "We've got to keep moving."

"But where *are* we?" she says. He doesn't like the look of her round the eyes.

"I don't know," he says and leads off again behind the dog.

A bit later Lorna's mare flounders sideways into a deep drift and he can't get her up. She lies heaving in the snow and doesn't blink when the flakes land on her open eye and begin to cover it. He rakes away snow and gets the girth buckle undone and pulls the bridle off over her ears and throws it in the snow.

"Come on," he says.

"No!" She's stroking away the snow that lands on her horse's neck.

"Come on!" And he grabs her by the shoulder of the coat and drags her onto her feet and away from the doomed horse. He gives her a grip on the gelding's tail. "Let that go and you've had it," he shouts in her ear, and they move off again.

Thirty or so yards away he stops. "I'd better go back and get that bridle," he tells Lorna. "You wait here."

He back-tracks to where her mare lies in the snow, already half-buried. He gets out his knife and cuts its throat and rejoins Lorna. "Can't find it," he says. "Let's keep going."

It's not much further on, or is it? He can't tell any more. Anyway she's not there now. He yells at Tash to stop and stumbles back along their tracks, already filling with snow. He finds her trying to get on her feet and he helps her up and walks her in front of him until they almost collide with the gelding with inches of snow on his rump. He gets her up into the saddle somehow, jams her feet into the stirrup leathers, gives her a handful of mane and tells the dog to get the hell moving.

They flounder on in a whiteness where he can't tell the ground from the sky, up from down. All he can see is the black on Tash bouncing along in front of him. He forgets exactly why he's following that irregular blob dancing along ahead, but he knows he has to keep doing it. Then the reins are pulled out of his hand and there's a thump behind him. He looks round in time to see the gelding on its front knees and Lorna just tipping off over its neck. He picks her up and stands her on her feet. The gelding stands up, its head drooping to the snow with exhaustion. It's just about wind broken. The Doughroaster looks at the horse there and reckons it's a bloody shame this has to happen to an animal with that much guts. And Tash is lying on his side in the snow panting.

Things don't look too good to The Doughroaster. Lorna wants to fall on the snow so he lets her go and he stumbles a few clumsy paces away to try and concentrate on what to do next. It's hard for him to think properly; his brains have gone like soap that's been left in the water. He holds out his hand and watches the big snowflakes immediately begin to cover it. Strange how something so gentle can be so deadly. He can't even feel it on his hand but it's going to kill them . . . slowly he realises that he's looking past his hand at the top eighteen inches of a post. He knows that post. He stapled this wire onto it. It's a gatepost – the gate into the holding paddock at Bullock Creek.

He stumbles back to Lorna, nearly missing her and the horse, and goes onto his knees beside her.

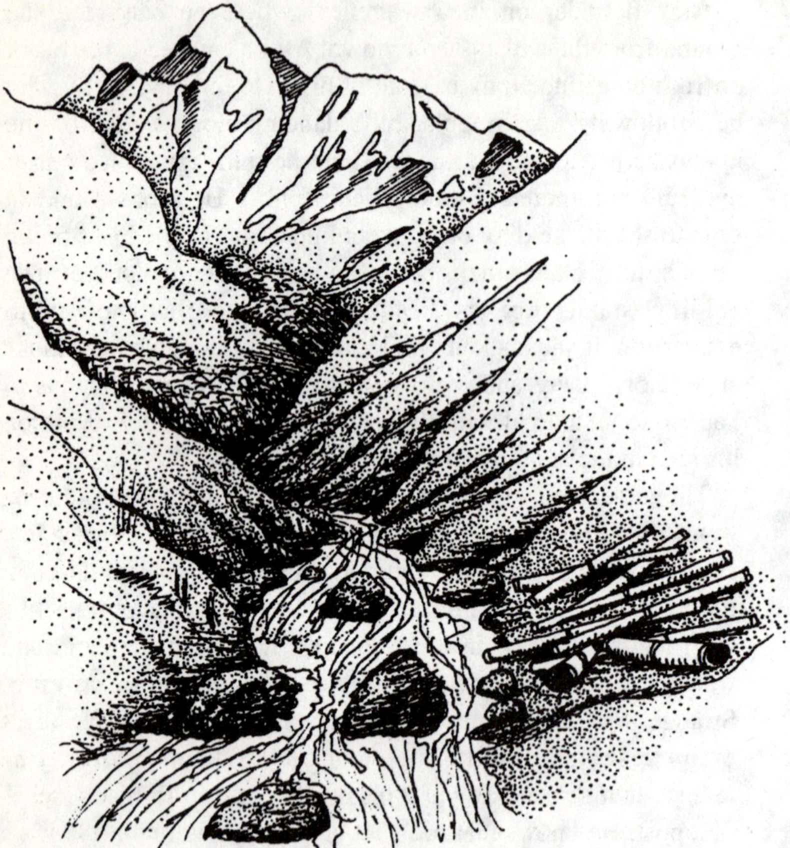

"We're there," he shouts, shaking her. "We're there! The holding-paddock gate's just over there. Come on! "I'll show you!"

She doesn't seem to be as interested as she ought to be, but he gets her standing up and holding a stirrup-leather and then kicks Tash till he gets on his feet. He gets the gelding to move off after him and they flounder through the holding-paddock gate and along the fence towards the homestead.

Lorna falls and he gets her up again and shoves her arm through the strirrup-leather. He'd like to help her more but even the reins are getting too heavy for him now. They move a few more yards and the horse stops. She's fallen again and dragging under its back feet. He gets them going again without knowing how he does it, and then forgets what they're doing until the shed looms up right in front of him. He leads the horse round to the doors. Lorna falls down. He gets the doors open and slaps the horse inside. There's no way he could undo buckles with these hands; the saddle and bridle will have to stay on for now.

He gets Lorna on her feet and they totter and crawl the sixty yards up to the house. He gets the door open and lays her on the floor and tries the phone. It's dead. He fumbles the plug into the bath and, using both hands, gets the taps turned on. The power's off but there's still hot water in the cylinder. When the bath's half-full of what seems to him like warm water he drags Lorna through from the kitchen and rolls her into the bath, clothes, boots and all. Then he sits against the bath with his hands in the water until some feeling begins to come back into them. They've been home for nearly an hour before he can get his coat and boots off.

Lorna's managed to get her gloves off and she's looking and talking a bit better by now, but she's still weak and shaking so he runs more hot water and tells her to stay there while he lights the fire and makes a cup of tea. Then he sits with his feet in the bath while they drink it. He has to help her out of the bath and get her boots and coat off. Then they fumble off to their rooms with towels to get into dry clothes.

They sit huddled up to the fire on the couch all night, only moving to put on more wood or make more tea. By morning they're still deep-down cold, but they're alive. And it's three days before they're getting back to normal.

The snow doesn't last long on the flats. A rain comes and turns most of it into slush in a day and two nights, and brings the river up sixteen feet, which takes two chain of fence off the corner of the holding-paddock.

The Doughroaster and Lorna are sitting in the homestead kitchen listening to the roaring of the water cascading down the hillsides, and Lorna says, "I've made up my mind, Barney. It's not worth trying to hold on here any more. I'm going to get in touch with Johnny Knight and tell him he can have the place, if his offer still stands."

"You'd never be pleased you gave up like that," says The Doughroaster. "After all you've put into the place."

"I don't care any more. It's just not worth risking our lives for. We could have died in that snow."

"That's not going to happen again," he says. "It's only a matter of holding out till the thaw now. If we can make it through to the summer I reckon you've got a good chance of selling the place for what it's worth."

"But is it worth risking our lives for? Nobody can stand up against the sort of weather we're having. And all the poor sheep out in the snow, and now this rain."

"They can take it," he tells her. "They're merinos. I think we ought to hang on a bit longer and see if the weather improves."

"We can't move until this rain stops and the river goes down again anyway," she sighs. "But it does get me down at times."

On the first fine day The Doughroaster saddles the gelding and rides out and quarters the flats until he finds where Lorna's mare is lying, still half-buried in a patch of snow in a stony hollow, about three hundred and fifty yards from the holding-paddock gate. He has to tie the saddle onto the gelding's tail to drag it out from under the carcass. He finds the bridle a few yards away and before he leaves he throws a layer of rocks and stones over the dead horse, in case Lorna comes across it.

Back at the shed he cleans up Lorna's saddle and bridle and hangs them up where they usually go. Then he catches the spare gelding and rides it round a bit to check it out and then tacks a set of shoes on it for her. It's not a bad horse. A bit lazy, but easy to catch and hard to frighten. Been someone's pet, by the way it behaves.

He gets Lorna to ride out with him to check the sheep, to take her mind off quitting, and it seems to be working. They've lost only about forty sheep, mostly ewes, cast and smothered in hollows, and The Doughroaster marvels again at the endurance of merino sheep.

Lorna's handling the loss of her horse better than he'd have thought; she was pretty fond of that horse. She seems to have transferred all her affection onto Tash, who she's convinced saved their lives that day. The Doughroaster knows that his fitness and the fitness of his horse had just as much to do with it, and he doesn't approve of all this mollycoddling of dogs, but he shudders when he thinks how close they came that day to being found dead at their own holding-paddock gatepost.

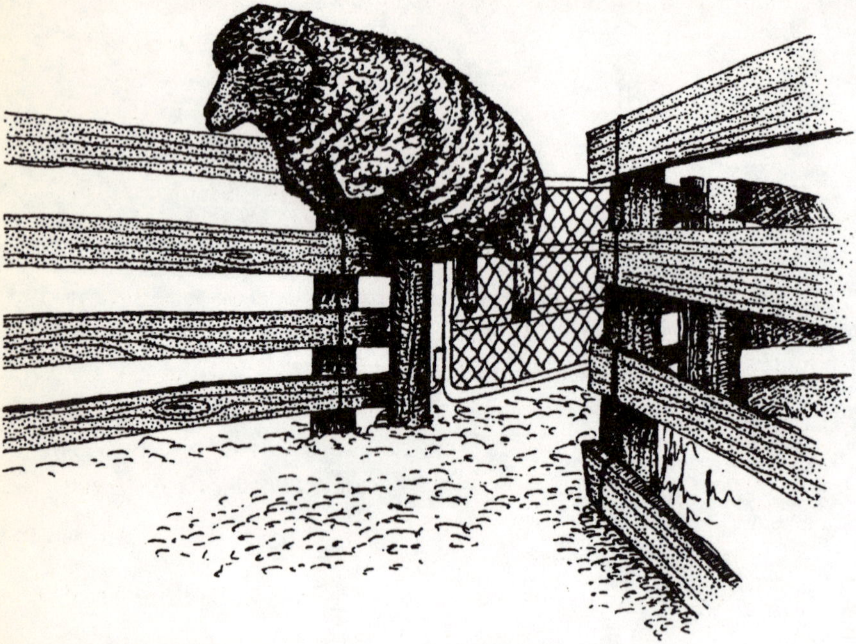

EIGHT

THE WANDERING WETHERS

It's the worst winter anyone round here can remember. No one's seen this much snow here before. Doubleburn's already lost two hundred of their ewes, buried in the snow. Mangatane, they hear, hasn't fared so badly, with plenty of open country. With at least six weeks to go before he can begin to hope for an early thaw, The Doughroaster watches the grazing vanish and the sheep getting hungrier and harder to keep away from deep snow, foraging for feed.

He leans against the doorway of the shed and watches the showers of powder-snow blown up into the air off the rim of a ridge and wonders how he's going to keep the sheep alive.

He walks in thought up to the house for lunch. Mutton and bread.

"They'll lose condition real quick unless we can get some tucker into them," he tells Lorna.

"Could we buy some, do you think?"

"No, there won't be a bale of hay for sale within a hundred miles of here."

"What can we do then?"

"I've been thinking, if we could get the rest of the wethers off the place we could probably get the ewes through to the thaw."

"The rest of the wethers?"

"Er, yeah," says The Doughdodger. "They're grazing a few of them on Mangatane for us for a favour."

"That's nice of them, but what are we going to do with the rest? Could we sell them?"

The Doughroaster shakes his head, "We couldn't give them away right now. The nearest grass I know of is down on the foothills. We could stick 'em out on the road and let 'em graze in that direction."

"Will they be safe?"

"No, but they've got a better chance of surviving out there than starving here. It'd give us a breather, and we should get some of them back. They're all ear-tagged."

"It doesn't look as though we've got much option, does it?"

"We haven't."

So he musters the remaining eight hundred and eighty wethers and pushes them across the river and out onto the road. The river is low but he still loses four weak ones in the crossing. He rides down the river after a floating drowning sheep and reaches down and lifts it up by the head and cuts its throat for dog-tucker and leaves it kicking feebly on the bank. Then he heads the mob out towards the foothills and they begin hungrily leapfrogging up the roadsides.

The idea doesn't come to him until he notices that a bunch of the wethers, about three hundred of them, has branched off up the Mangatane Road. It's too unplanned and risky and he's only trying to see how far he can get, but he rides ahead of the three hundred wethers towards Mangatane and lets the dog bring them along behind him. If anyone comes up the road he only has to turn round and be taking this bunch of strays back to Bullock Creek. The tricky bit's going to be what to do with them if he does get them there without being seen.

It takes him five hours to cover the eleven miles. He has to finish off a few weak sheep and hide them in the scrub away from the road. He makes it without being seen by anyone and it's getting on towards dark. There's already a light on up at the homestead. And here's a bit of luck. They've brought their in-lamb ewes out onto the front country because of the snow. The wethers wont be so conspicuous among them and they'll be tricky to separate.

He stops the mob and sits on his horse in a scrubby hollow and waits for it to get a bit darker. Tash knows they're doing something a bit sneaky and he tip-toes around the sheep in a stealthy way that makes even The Doughroaster grin. Being sprung by the Mangatane dogs is his main worry now and he tells his dog to shut up every now and then in case he's even thinking of making any noise.

When it's dark enough they move the wethers quietly and slowly across Mangatane's Road Paddock and through a gate onto the tussock faces among the ewes. It's a nervous ride back down the road to Bullock Creek and although he makes it without being spotted, The Doughroaster's a bit uneasy about this operation. He's left a trail of hoofprints through every patch of snow and mud up both sides of the road between Bullock Creek and Mangatane, and for the first time in his life he watches anxiously for a fresh fall of snow. He gets it two nights later and relaxes.

He spreads the ewes out through all the available grazing and keeps in touch with the wandering wethers in the ute every two or three days. Within a week they're fifteen miles away out in the foothills, scattered everywhere. The farmers out there are becoming familiar with the wandering Bullock Creek wethers and they aren't popular.

In the middle of all this The Doughroaster gets a visit from The Culprit. He comes lurking around the corner of the shed where The Doughroaster's stacking firewood, wet to above his knees from the river crossing. His old bomb is parked on the other side. The Doughroaster smells booze on him.

"What can I do for you, Culprit?"

"Just dropped by for a bit of a chat,' says The Culprit.

"What about?"

"Wethers."

"What about 'em?"

"I know who put all the wethers in with Jake's ewes."

"That a fact?"

"It was you. I saw you. I was in the woolshed. Jake's going to go crackers when he finds out. He's gone over to the coast for a few days."

"What about it?" says The Doughroaster.

"I ought to tell Jake when he gets back."

"Why haven't you told him already?"

"I thought I'd just see you first."

"What for?"

"I thought it might be worth something to keep quiet about."

"It might be, to you."

"To me? You're the one who put the wethers in there. I saw you."

"If I was Jake I'd want to know why you didn't tell me at the time. And if he finds out you've been over here wanting to know what it's worth not to tell him at all – he'll probably sack you on the spot. That's what I'd do."

"I was only trying to save you getting into trouble," says The Culprit.

"Do you want to know how to save yourself from getting into worse trouble?"

"How?"

"Get the hell out of here real quick. And if you want to hang onto your job on Mangatane I'd keep my mouth shut if I was you."

The Culprit scuttles off. Hard to say which way a bloke like him might go. The Doughroaster wonders again why Jake would want to keep someone like The Culprit around him. He shrugs and goes back to stacking firewood.

The Doughroaster's getting quite familiar with the telephone these days. Both his sons, Derek and Chris, have rung up to ask advice they don't really need but really to keep in touch with him. And Susie, home from boarding school, rings. He's been expecting a call from Ross on Doubleburn, but when he picks up the phone it's Susie. He doesn't know what to say.

" I miss you Dad." He hears her voice coming faintly through the wires and The Doughroaster feels a pang of nostalgia or something.

"I miss you too, Sweetheart," he says, looking around to see if Lorna can hear.

"When are you coming home?"

"Pretty soon," he says.

"When?"

"As soon as I've finished what I have to do down here."

"When will that be?"

"It's hard to say. Could be some time early in the summer. The year won't be up till then."

"Never mind the stupid year, Daddy. We miss you."

"Yeah, I know."

"Come home as soon as possible."

"Sure. As soon as possible."

"Sooner!"

"Okay, Love. I'd better go now."

"Ring and let us know when you're coming."

"Yeah, I'll do that. I'd better get off this phone in case someone wants to use it. It's a party line here."

"Did you get my letter?"

"Yeah. A couple of days ago."

"What did you think of my school report?"

"Well I haven't actually got round to reading your letter yet. It's in my ute across the river and we've got a bit of a flood on at the moment."

"Well don't forget to write."

"Sure Sweetheart. I'll get round to it one of these days."

They ramble on talking like this for quite a while before The Doughroaster gets himself off the phone. He likes his daughter. She can make him do just about anything.

But most of the phone calls he gets are from irate citizens out in the foothills and even in the outskirts of the town, forty miles away. It seems as though everyone out there has left the gates into their driveways, gardens, paddocks and crops open, and the wandering Bullock Creek wethers are up to their bellies in grass, flowers, vegetables and crops, and the owners of the grass, flowers, vegetables and crops aren't at all happy about it.

And he's running out of excuses – A flood took the road fence away – Hunters left one of our gates open and we've only just discovered it – A sheep-crate came off the back of a truck . . . And the response is always the same: "Sorry to hear that, mate, but come and get them off my place right now."

They keep both Lorna's waggon and The Doughroaster's ute on the other side of the river because when it's only a bit flooded he can get across to the road on the gelding. And he's doing quite a bit of that lately, in response to angry demands that he come and get bunches of his sheep off people's places and move them somewhere else. It's no use bringing them back to Bullock Creek to starve, so he shifts them up different roads and leaves them there until someone else complains. He only knows where about half the wethers are at the moment, but any old ring of the telephone is likely to tell him in no uncertain terms where a few more of them can be found.

And now he's about to find out about the progress of another of his slightly unorthodox farming initiatives. Lorna calls him up to the house to take yet another call from an irate farmer.

"It's Johnny Knight," she whispers, handing him the phone. "He seems to be upset about something."

The Doughroaster gets on the phone.

"That you, Doughroaster?" barks Jake.

"Yeah. What can I do for you?"

"How the hell did all those cross-bred wethers of yours get in among my ewes?"

So The Culprit hasn't told him.

"Yeah? How many?"

"Bloody dozens of them."

"Well just draft them out and I'll come over and get them."

"I can't muster now, it's too close to lambing!"

"That's right," agrees The Doughroaster. "We'd just about have to wait till you do your docking before we can sort them out now, wouldn't we."

"That's bloody weeks away! In the meantime I'm feeding out to your mongrel bloody wethers. How the hell did they get in there, and what are you going to do about it?"

"We'll have to check that boundary of ours come summer, and find out where all these sheep and cattle are getting through onto your place."

"What cattle are you talking about?" says Jake uneasily.

"We're missing a few head of cattle as well. Sixty-odd cows and calves and nine steers."

"I don't know anything about your cattle. They're not over here."

"Well you'd know if they were, wouldn't you? Yours are all pure Black-Polls and ours have got Hereford in them. And Doubleburn's are all Shorthorn-cross, so you'd . . ."

"Shut up about your bloody cattle, will you. I've told you they're not here. Now what the hell are you going to do about these wethers?"

"What do you want me to do about them?"

"Well you could at least pay me for some of the tucker they're eating."

"You're feeding it to them," points out The Doughroaster.

"They've got in with my ewes, eating their bloody heads off!"

"Sorry about that. I'll come over and get them as soon as they're drafted out."

"You won't get away with this, Doughroaster. You'll be getting an account for fifteen bags of sheep-nuts."

"Sheep-nuts? That's getting a bit extravagant, isn't it?"

Jake has hung up.

"What's the matter with him?" asks Lorna. "He sounded quite angry."

"Nothing much. He wanted to keep some of our stock on his place so I let him. Now he wants to back out of the deal, but he can't, and he doesn't like it."

"Oh, I hope he doesn't stop talking to us over it."

"There's no need to worry about that," says The Doughroaster. "We'll be hearing plenty from Jake. We've got more business to do with him yet."

"What sort of business?" asks Lorna.
"Mainly to do with the stock," he says vaguely.

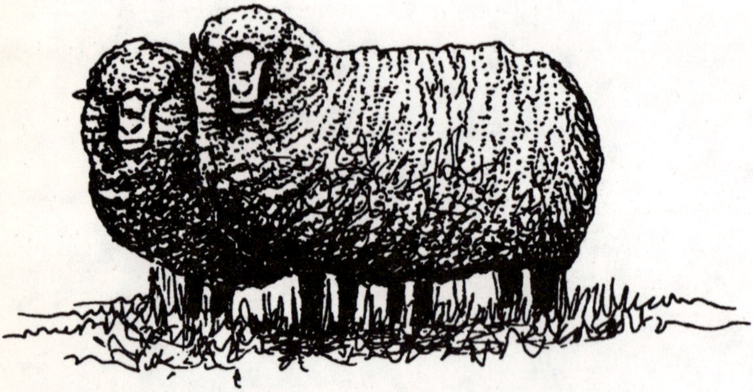

NINE
A FAIR PRICE

The doughroaster's being kept fairly busy sorting out problems connected with the wandering wethers, and it's just as well he's the only one around the house when Jake rings up again, about a fortnight after the first time. And he's sounding angry again.

"What the hell do you think you're playing at, Doughroaster?"

"What's wrong now?"

"All those wethers of yours among mine up on my winter block. There must be four or five hundred of them!"

"So *that's* where they got to! I've been thinking of reporting them stolen."

"Cut it out, Doughroaster, you knew bloody well they were there. You probably put them there, you cunning old bastard! There must be a thousand of your bloody sheep on my place!"

"Settle down, mate," says The Doughroaster. "I tried to get our stock off your place months ago, and you wouldn't even let me on to look for them. And now you're going crook about them being there!"

"I had no idea there were that many of them. I'm overstocked to hell on that winter block now, with all this bloody snow and your bloody sheep."

"Well just draft them out and I'll come over and get them," says The Doughroaster helpfully.

"You know bloody well I can't muster up there in these conditions."

"That's right, never thought of that. Looks like we'll have to wait till it thaws. Why don't we leave it till you do your docking and I'll come over and give you a hand to sort out all our sheep and cattle in one go."

"Meantime I suppose I go on feeding all your mongrel bloody wethers."

"Looks like it," sympathises The Doughroaster.

"I'll shoot the bloody things!"

"You wouldn't want to do that,' says The Doughroaster. "I've got an idea it's a pretty serious crime, shooting your neighbours' stock."

"Well what the hell am I supposed to do with them? I'm going to have to buy-in more feed now."

"We're going to have to get stuck in and do something about that boundary fence of ours this summer, by the look of things."

"I'll be doing something about more than the boundary fence, mate. That place won't see another season out, I promise you that. If it wasn't for you she'd have been off there by now, but you won't last much longer. I'll see to that!"

"The place is for sale," The Doughroaster reminds him.

"I wouldn't buy that run-down dump at any price," snarls Jake. "And I'm getting legal advice about your stock running all over my place. You're not getting away with this!"

And he slams down the phone.

The Doughroaster forgets about Jake until a week later, when Jake's Land Cruiser bounces across the river in an angry shower of spray and jerks to a stop beside The Doughroaster where he's come out of the shed.

"All right, Doughroaster, what the hell's the idea?"

"What's the matter this time?" asks The Doughroaster innocently.

"You know bloody well what's the matter – how the hell did all those cattle of yours get on my place?"

"Have you got our cattle over there as well? No wonder we haven't been able to find them. Just as well you told me. We've been thinking of going to the police about all the stock that's been going missing off this place."

"Don't hand me that, you shifty old bastard. I don't know how you did it but you put all those sheep and cattle on my place, I know you did."

"All you have to do is round 'em up and I'll come over and get 'em," says The Doughroaster reasonably.

"You can't ride that country in the winter, and I'm damned if I'm mustering bloody cattle on foot."

"Well if you can't get 'em in you can't very well expect me to. Looks like they'll have to stay there till the spring now."

"What the bloody hell are they doing there in the first place?" demands Jake. "That's what I want to know."

"Short of grass," says The Doughroaster truthfully.

"You can't go sticking your stock on other people's places just because you're short of bloody grass. I can have you for that."

"You wouldn't want to do that," says The Doughroaster.

"Don't you believe it. I've had a gutsful of you. You've just about ruined me this winter, sticking all your stock on my place."

"Saves you helping yourself though, doesn't it."

"What the hell do you mean by that?"

"Come on Jake, you were getting careless by the time I turned up around here. You've been flogging beef and wool off Bullock Creek and Doubleburn for years. Any good stockman could tell what's going on over on your place."

"I can't help it if a bit of stray stock wanders onto my property from time to time," says Jake with a flicker of the eyes.

"A thousand sheep and seventy head of cattles takes a bit more explaining away than that, me old mate," says The Doughroaster. "It's a pretty serious crime, sheep and cattle stealing."

"You put that stuff on there, you shifty old bastard, and I'm not letting you get away with it. I'm going to lay charges with the police."

"You reckon they'd believe you?"

"Of course they will. I've had legal advice about it."

"You'll have to try and convince them that Ross Nathan sneaked all the Doubleburn stock onto your place as well,' observes The Doughroaster.

"What Doubleburn stock?"

"Give it up Jake. I know every gully on your place and every head of stock on it. You've got at least thirty-six head of Bullock Creek-bred cattle over there with your earmark cut over the top of ours – in the wrong part of the ear. And you've got quite a few Doubleburn Shorthorn-crosses, as well as about a hundred of their ewes. You're in no position to go running to the police about anything."

"I told you to keep off Mangatane," snarls Jake.

"I don't always do what I'm told."

"I could have you up for trespass."

"You could, if you could catch me trespassing."

"Look Doughroaster, what's your game? What are you trying to get out of all this?"

"A fair price for Bullock Creek. Give her what she's asking for it."

"Come on mate, it'd take me years to get my money back."

"Not if the flats have got as much gold in them as I think there is," says The Doughroaster.

"Who have you been talking to?"

"No one. I know you're into gold-mining and there's only one reason on earth why anyone'd want this place, and it isn't for farming. This was one of the richest spots in Otago in the gold-rush days. It's not hard to figure that one out."

"You're pretty damn smart, aren't you."

"Yeah."

Jake is exasperated. He slaps the bonnet of his Cruiser hard with the flat of his hand.

"Look Doughroaster, I'll tell you. I would have bought this place. I wanted it. There's no money in farming but there could be good gold in these flats. I was jacking up the operation here with a couple of partners I've got in a claim over on the Coast. We're just about cut-out over there, but this place is no good to us now."

"How come?"

"We didn't want to put in for a Prospecting Licence before we bought the station in case someone woke up to us. As the owner of the land, Lorna Fletcher could have blocked us under the new Mining Act and held out for more money. Mining licences don't just grow on trees, you know. And now some hoon called Woods has taken out a prospecting licence on the place ahead of us."

"I know," says The Doughroaster.

"How do you know that?"

"Because it was me. I'm Henry Woods."

"You mean you hold the prospecting rights to Bullock Creek?"

"Yeah. I applied for it after I had a look at what you've got in your implement shed over at Mangatane."

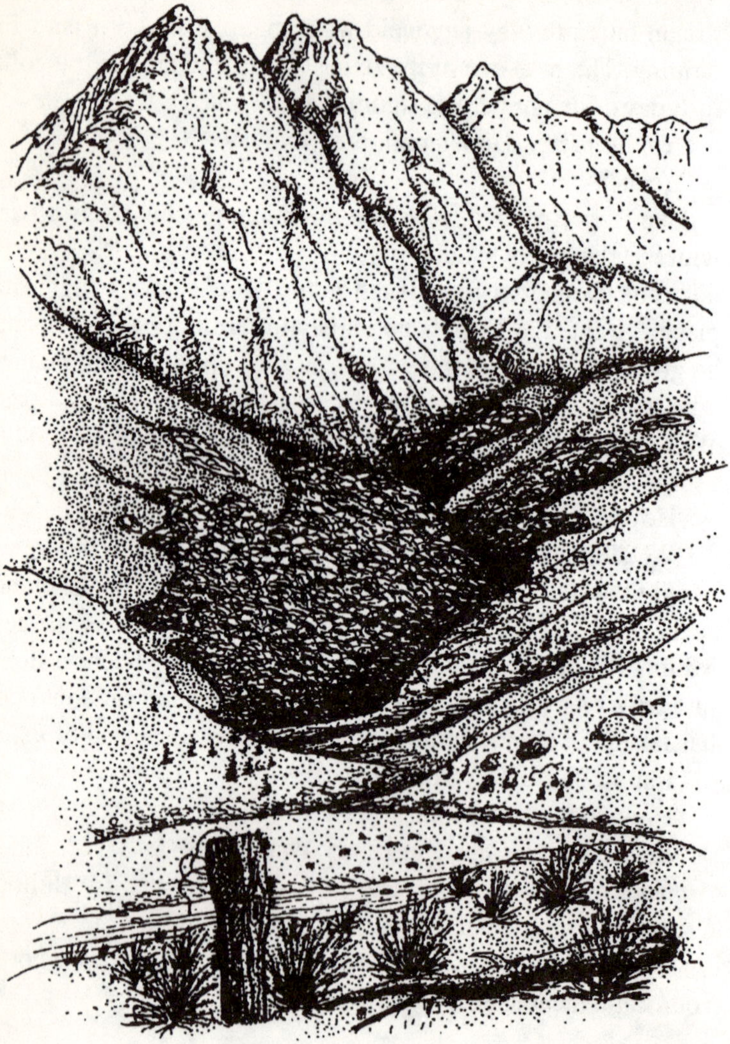

"Well I'll go to hell, you crafty old bastard. You've been setting me up!"

"It's you who's been trying to set people up," The Doughroaster reminds him. "This place is still on the market, at Lorna Fletcher's price."

"Does the prospecting licence go with the deal?"

"For an extra fifteen thousand dollars."

"You thieving old bastard!"

"You can talk!"

"I don't know. I'll have to consult with my partners."

Jake's trying not to let on how interested he is. "I'll have to let you know," he says, getting into his waggon.

"You've got a week," The Doughroaster tells him.

"Then what?"

"The place goes on the open market, prospecting rights and all."

"You wouldn't."

"Try me."

Jake drives off, muttering.

"Was that Jake you were talking to down there?" asks Lorna.

"Yeah."

"You should have invited him up for a cup of tea. He must think we're awfully rude."

"He was in a bit of a hurry," says The Doughfibber. "Said to tell you he'll catch up with you next time."

"What did he come for?"

"We were discussing the stock, mainly, but I think he might be getting serious about wanting to buy this place off you."

"He'd have to come up with a better price than he offered last time."

"You'll get your price," predicts The Doughroaster.

Jake doesn't waste any time. Three days later The Doughroaster comes in from the sheep and Lorna says, "Guess what!"

"What?"

"Jake rang up a little while ago. He sounded very nice on the phone. He's coming over with his lawyer tomorrow to discuss buying the station. He says he's sure we can come to an agreement, even after I told him I was sticking to my price."

"Good," says The Doughroaster, "but I reckon you ought to add about twenty thousands dollars onto that."

"What for?"

"The stock."

"Is it worth that much?"

"Sure. It's only a few bucks a head. He's getting a real good bargain at that."

"Really?"

"It's worth a go," he says.

"All right, I will. Just think of it, Barney. We've nearly made it through the winter and we might be selling the station!"

"There's a bit to be done yet," says The Doughroaster, "but we've been pretty lucky so far."

The next day Jake and two other men arrive to meet with Lorna in the homestead kitchen and spread paper and words everywhere. The Doughroaster, coming in from the sheep, sees them shaking hands at the gate and contrives to arrive at the homestead after they've gone. Lorna glows with excitement.

"We've made a deal" she tells him, squeezing his arm. "They were very nice about everything. I get my cheque paid into the bank by the end of November!"

"Did you get your price?"

"Yes. Two hundred thousand for the station, the buildings, the plant and the stock. Marvellous, isn't it! They take over on the first of December."

"Bloody good!"

"Don't swear. You know, Barney, I'm glad Jake's getting Bullock Creek. He's such a nice man when you get to know him. He *deserves* it."

"He sure does," agrees The Doughroaster.

"We've only got to sign it up now. They were hoping to see you. They said something about prospecting rights. What were they talking about?"

"Gold."

"Gold? What's gold got to do with it?"

"They're buying this place so they can work the flats for gold."

"How do you know?"

"I guessed."

"But how?"

"Whatever else Jake is, he knows a bit about high-country farming, and nobody who knows anything about high-country farming would take this place on at any price. I knew he'd made you an offer and when I found out he was interested in gold mining I took out a prospecting licence on Bullock Creek and waited for him to come up with the right price."

"The pig! He's been trying to swindle me all this time! He told me he wanted to add Bullock Creek to Mangatane for a wether-block."

"Don't worry about it. He's ended up having to pay more than he needed to, and now he has to pay me another fifteen thousand dollars for the prospecting rights."

"How on earth did you get him to agree to that?"

"We're good mates" says The Doughroaster.

His good mate comes back the next day to get Lorna to sign some legal papers and The Doughroaster to sign the prospecting rights to Bullock Creek over to something called Knight-Fenmore Ltd. He examines the cheque carefully before he signs the transfer. It's made out to H. Woods for fifteen thousand dollars.

"Thanks cobber," he says, folding the cheque and tucking it under the corner of the clock on the mantelpiece.

"Go to hell" snarls Jake, and he stuffs his papers into his briefcase and walks out of the house.

The Doughroaster follows Jake outside. He's running a bit late today, it's time to get round the stock. Jake's stopped by the gate.

"She doesn't even know what you've been up to, does she?" he says to The Doughroaster.

"Neither do you."

"Look, Doughroaster. What have you got against me? I've never done you any harm, have I."

"You've never been able to."

"Then why don't you lay off me? You've cost me thousands!"

"I just don't happen to like anyone who'd thieve off someone in Lorna Fletcher's situation. I'm a bit old-fashioned about things like that."

"Well she's got her deal now. How about getting off my back, eh?"

The Doughroaster shrugs. "Okay, but I want all our stock off Mangatane and back on here."

"Why? I'm buying it all anyway."

"Because up until the first of December I'm the manager of this station and I want all the stock on the place. It's a matter of principle."

"I'll be glad to get rid of the bloody stuff. Is that all you want?"

"Yeah."

Jake holds out his hand, "There we're quits?"

The Doughroaster hesitates and then shakes hands briefly.

"You're a hard bastard, Doughroaster."

"I'm only as hard as I need to be."

Jake drives off and The Doughroaster catches the gelding and rides off to check on the ewes. At dinner that night Lorna can talk about nothing but the selling of the station.

"What was wrong with Jake today?" she says. "He didn't even drink his cup of tea?"

"It's an old joke between us," says The Doughroaster. "Every time him and I do a deal he comes off second-best."

"Oh, I thought he was getting angry about something."

"Nar, not Jake. It's just his manner. He's as happy as a sand-boy."

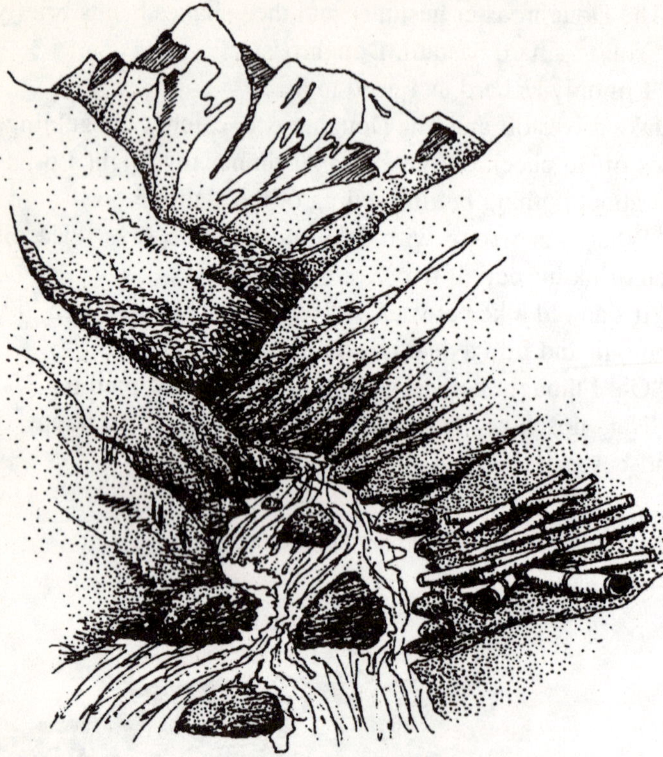

TEN

THE THAW

The thaw is here! Two days of weak sunshine – then a warm rain – a flood – more sun – snow melts into slush – mud – another flood – more mud . . . The sheep spread away up the slopes as the snow recedes and the tussocks and grasses start shooting. The first of the lambs appear and now even the weather can't deny it's spring.

They ring up from Mangatane to say that all the Bullock Creek sheep will be drafted-out and ready to be collected in about a week. Jake obviously doesn't want any more trouble with The Doughroaster. And they must be eating a lot of his new grass.

The Doughroaster handles the Bullock Creek cattle by phone. He tells Jake he's sending a cattle-truck to pick them up, and Jake agrees to get them in and loaded for him. And when they arrive at Bullock Creek he redirects them to the saleyards in Clinton. Next day he and Lorna go in to see them sold and return home just under eight thousand dollars better off.

"Those cows wintered pretty well, considering," says The Doughroaster on the way back.

"I hope Jake doesn't find out about us selling them," says Lorna. "He's supposed to be buying all the stock off us."

"Those cows weren't on Bullock Creek when he made the deal. It says on the agreement — all the stock on the property."

"Oh Barney, Ross Nathan's right about you. He says you're as sharp as a sack-needle and as tough as a wool-pack."

"Garn!"

And they smile.

It takes him nearly two weeks to find five hundred of the wandering wethers and get them back on Bullock Creek, bunches at a time. They've lost about eighty of them, including seventeen they know about but are not worth redeeming from the pound in town. Some of the farmers out in the foothills are hanging onto the wethers until damage or grazing is paid for. It costs The Doughroaster sixteen hundred dollars to settle all the claims he can't talk them out of. He sells one bunch of eight to a lady who's grown fond of them. It's been a lot of mucking around and hassle, but he's saved a lot of sheep from dying of starvation.

"I just don't know how to thank you, Barney" says Lorna as they watch the last bunch of wanderers he's brought back spread out feeding across the flats beyond the woolshed. "I know I wouldn't have been able to get through this winter without you."

"That'd be right," agrees The Doughroaster.

"I'm going to pay you for all the work you've done here when I get my money."

"I've got a better idea than that," says The Doughroaster.

"What's that?"

"We'll take the wool-clip before we leave here."

"Will that be enough?"

"Plenty."

"But isn't it Johnny Knight's wool? He's buying the place."

"He's buying the stock, but it doesn't say anything in the agreement about the wool. He won't say anything. He doesn't take over till December anyway."

"Let's do it then."

"The only thing is that I can't ask The Hog and Tommy to help. They're flat-out over on Doubleburn just now, and three

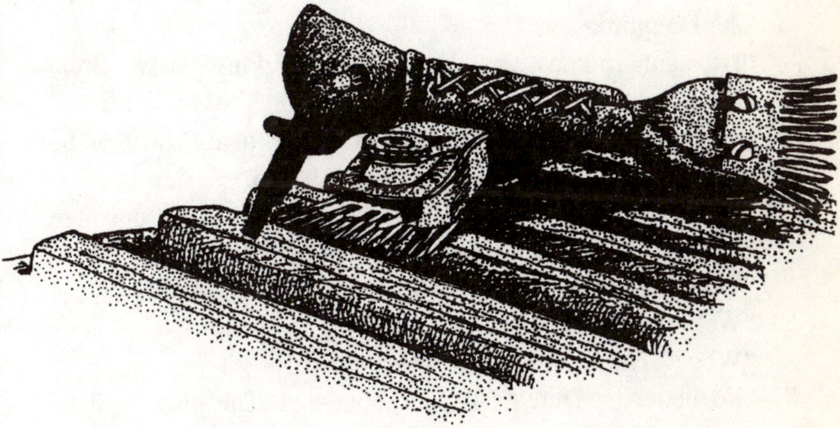

and-a-half thousand sheep's too many for me on my own. It'd take me too long."

"Why don't you get one of your boys to come down and help?"

"Nar," says The Doughroaster.

"Why not? They've offered several times."

"They're probably pretty busy themselves anyway."

"They wouldn't keep offering if they were too busy to come. I think you should let them help."

Lorna gets up from the table to answer the phone.

"It's Chris!" she calls out.

Lorna talks to him for a bit and smiles as she hands the phone to The Doughroaster.

"He wants to know if we've done the docking yet and if we need any help."

And so The Doughroaster has to admit to his son that he could use a bit of a hand to shear a few sheep.

"We'll both come," says Chris instantly. "Derek's not here just now, but I know he'll want to come."

"What about that place? Who's going to look after that?"

"We've got someone."

"Who?" The Doughroaster smells a rat.

"I'd better let Derek tell you about that. The place will be okay though."

He goes back into the kitchen feeling as though things have been taken out of his hands.

"Is he coming?" asks Lorna.

"Looks like they both might turn up,' says The Doughroaster. "They're going to ring back tonight and let us know when they're arriving."

"I'll get you to help me shift the spare bed into the other

room. Will they mind sharing a room, do you think?"

"Nar, they'll be right. I just hope they don't turn out to be a nuisance round the place."

"Don't be ridiculous, Barney. Now come and help me with this bed."

That evening The Doughroaster seems a bit nervous. The phone rings twice for other things before Derek gets through. They seem to have it all organised.

"All you've got to do is meet us off the Road Services bus in Clinton at half past two next Thursday, the twelfth. You got that, Dad?"

"Yeah, I'll be there. You'd better bring your own handpieces. We've only got one here."

"Okay. Anything else you need?"

"No, I don't think so."

"How many have you got to shear?"

"About three-and-a-half thousand. Ewes and wethers."

"That won't take us long to cut-out."

"It might take a bit longer than you think," says The Doughroaster.

"Why's that?"

"These are merinos."

"What's the difference?"

"Ar – you'll find out. They're just a bit tricky to get the hang of, that's all."

"Well we'll see you the day after tomorrow then."

"Sure."

"We've all missed you, Dad. It'll be good to see you again."

"Sure. See you then."

"Okay, see you."

An air of expectation at Bullock Creek. Lorna spring cleans

the house. The Doughroaster butchers fresh mutton. They compile a list of supplies and Lorna adds biscuits and fruit to the list.

They go in early to town, both of them, and do their shopping, and they're waiting at the bus terminal when the bus swings in. Chris gets off with his bag, Derek follows him, and then Susie – his whole family gets off the bus. The Doughroaster is blown away. He can hardly speak at first.

"This is Mrs Fletcher," he says shaking hands with his sons. Susie's got him by the other arm. "This is Derek, and Chris, and this is Susie."

Lorna shakes hands with the boys and gives Susie a brief hug.

Derek's twenty now. Tall and serious and thin, and unmistakably Barney's son when you see them both together. Chris, at eighteen, is still very boyish and exuberant, unaware of his good looks and the cheekiness of his grin. You can see that Derek's in the habit of keeping his young brother under control. And Susie, twelve and pretty and still hanging onto her dad's arm. She's been missing him all right.

"Aren't you supposed to be at school?" he says.

"We drove up and got her," says Derek.

And The Doughroaster knows not to argue about it. He knows how hard it is to get anyone out of that boarding-school without a damn good reason. The boys must have been pretty persuasive. This all leaves the poor old Doughroaster a bit numb and clumsy. It's Lorna who gets them moving.

They crowd into Lorna's waggon among the boxes and bags of supplies and head off for Bullock Creek. None of The Doughroaster's family has been in the South Island before and there's quite a bit of excited chatter from Susie and Chris as they get deeper into the mountainous environs of Bullock Creek. But they're silent when they pull up at the Bullock Creek crossing.

"Is this where you live, Dad?" says Chris, looking as though hypnotised at the tumbledown old homestead across the river.

"Yeah, why?"

Susie looks up at the gaunt misty peaks of the Barker Range and says, "Gosh, Dad!"

"Gosh what?"

"You actually *farm* that country?" says Derek.

"Yeah. It's not as bad as it looks," says The Doughroaster.

"And you *live* there?"

"I've been living here for nearly five years now," says Lorna.

"Wow!" says Chris. "How do we get across that river?"

The Doughroaster, lost for words, has a look at the crossing and decides to risk driving across and just makes it. They unload the waggon and the gelding's hanging around so The Doughroaster saddles him and gets Derek to drive the waggon over the river and doubles him back, because the weather doesn't look the best. By the time they get back to the house Chris has the fire started, Lorna has the tea mugs and bread and cold mutton on the table, and Susie has Peterkin the cat purring on her lap. And it's just starting to rain.

And so the old Bullock Creek homestead comes alive with the talk and laughter of young people. Everyone's pleased to be here, and that night the Barker Range turns on a good hefty storm for them. They sit round the fire listening to the snarling sheets of rain being blown against the old house. Lorna gets the buckets from the porch and puts them under where the roof leaks. The youngsters seem a bit nervous as the gusts grow stronger and tear and rattle and shake the old building. There's a crash outside and they crowd to the doorway to see the water-tank being blown rumbling and drumming along the fenceline

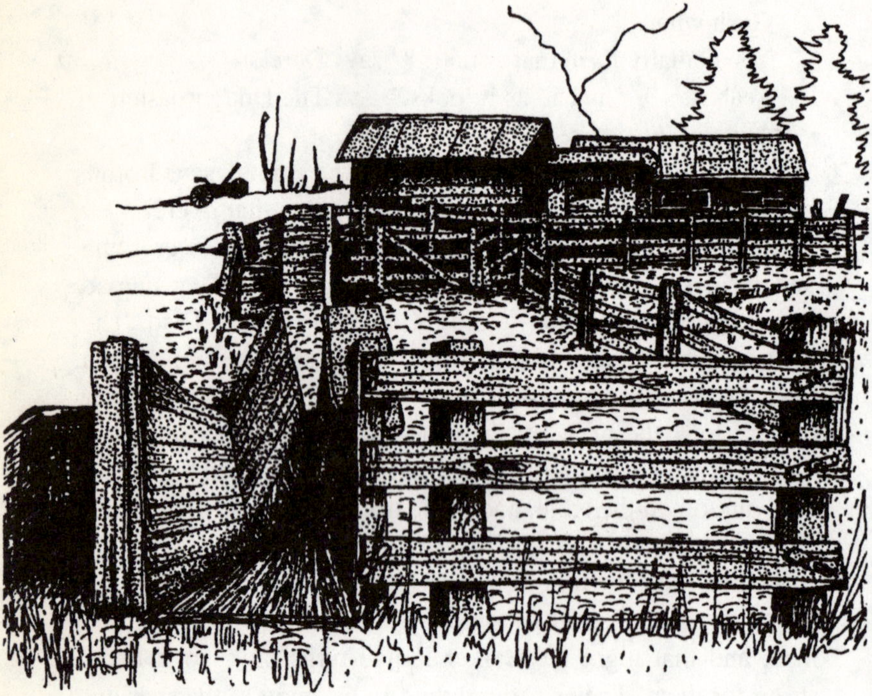

and out into the darkness of the holding-paddock.

"What was that?" says Chris.

"The water-tank," says The Doughroaster.

"Does that mean we've got no water?" says Susie.

"No, we've got a pipe into a spring up the hill. There was no water in the tank anyway. The last bit of wind we had here took away most of the guttering."

"Wow!" says Chris, which seems to be his favourite word just now.

They return to their chairs around the fire.

"Do you get much of this kind of weather here?" asks Derek, raising his voice above the roaring of the gale and the sound of the water splashing into the buckets off the ceiling.

"Quite a bit," says Lorna, shaking out wool, and she and The Doughroaster glance across the room at one another and smile their private memory of the winter they've just come through.

The storm is in full surge next day and all they can do is stay inside and stoke up the fire and wait it out. Susie stands holding the cat, looking out the window at the weather-shredded slopes of the Barker Range, streaming white with cascading rainwater and melted snow. "There's a whole waterfall being blown away in the wind up on the mountain," she says.

"Yes, love," says Lorna without looking up from her knitting.

"How do you get in and out when the river's up like this?" asks Derek.

"You don't," says The Doughroaster.

"What do you do?" says Chris.

"You stay put until it goes down again."

There's been something on The Doughroaster's mind.

"Who've you got looking after the farm up there?" he asks Derek.

"Jean."

"That girlfriend of yours?"

"Yep."

"Does she know what she's doing?"

"She ought to. She's been living with us for five months and working on the place. She likes it."

"Yeah?"

"They're getting married," says Susie, still looking out the window holding the cat.

"They're what?"

"We're hoping to get married as soon as you get back," says Derek. "Before Christmas, if possible."

The Doughroaster's a bit stonkered.

"What do the Pearsons think about it?" he says.

"They're all for it," says Chris. "You're the only one who's been missing."

"Mrs Pearson's already given them heaps of stuff," says Susie.

"You don't need me to get married," says The Doughroaster. "You could have gone ahead and done it."

"No, Dad," says Derek. "We want you there. You'll be home before Christmas, won't you?"

"Could be."

"Then we can go ahead and plan the wedding for mid-December?"

"I might be finished up here by then," he admits.

"Come on, Dad. We've got to know for sure."

"I'm not that keen on weddin's and things," he says. "What am I supposed to do, anyway?"

"Nothing. You just have to be there."

"I suppose I could handle that."

"Then you'll be there?"

"I suppose so," he says.

The storm blows itself out during the night and next day is more or less fine, but everything's still too wet and soggy for them to start mustering. Chris borrows Lorna's horse and rides out with The Doughroaster to have a look at the extent of the damage. They find the water-tank wedged in rocks a quarter of a mile from the homestead, distorted beyond repair. A slip has taken a fairly big section out of the track round to Boundary Creek, adding a ten-minute detour to the ride. The river's changed course in several places but they've been lucky with it this time. They find six wethers standing on an island of tussock in a shallow lake of floodwater and decide they'll be all right there till the floodwaters drain away in a day or two.

Derek does a bit of work around the woolshed and Lorna teaches Susie how to use the spinning-wheel. They've cooked a big meal of roast mutton and spuds and boiled cabbage, and there's plenty of talk at the dinner table.

"Wait till you see the woolshed," Derek says to Chris. "It came out of the Ark!"

"Wait till you see the *sheep*," says Chris. "They were in the Ark!"

"How do you muster all that country with only one dog?" Derek asks The Doughroaster.

"The sheep round here come when they're called."

"Do they?" says Susie.

"No," says Derek. "He's having us on."

"He gets help," guesses Chris.

"No,' says Lorna. "Barney musters all our country with Tash on his own."

She likes to get a plug in for Tash whenever she can.

Two days later they start to muster everything down off the higher faces. It takes them five days to get them all into the holding-paddock, which Derek has been working on the fences of.

"That dog of the old man's is a champion," The Doughroaster overhears Chris tell Derek. "He just tells it to go and get the sheep and it does, from miles away. The old man just sits on his horse and waits for them. And you want to see the places he rides that horse of his! You wouldn't believe it unless you saw it yourself!"

By the time they've mustered in all the sheep the champion dog has worn himself and his feet out again, but this time he's got two ladies fussing over him. And The Doughroaster's got two ladies telling him what a mean brute he is for working poor Tash so hard. Even the dog seems to look disapprovingly at him from under Susie's protective arm.

It's a three-stand shed. The Doughroaster shows his boys the tricks of handling and shearing the wrinkly merinos and they get stuck into it. The ladies yard-up and do the fleeces, and the men take it in turns to knock-off shearing and press the bales of wool. It doesn't start raining again until they've got the last shedful of sheep in, and in eight back-breaking days they've finished the lot, sixty-two-and-a-half bales of wool. They let the sheep find their own way back out onto the block because the women still won't let The Doughroaster use his dog. They decide to take it easy for a day or two.

It's a quiet evening after dinner. The dishes are done, the wind's dropped and it's only raining lightly. The Doughroaster sits looking into the fire. Lorna knits in the opposite chair. Chris and Susie are on the sofa, Chris reading and Susie stroking the cat. Derek has his shearing handpiece in pieces on newspaper on the table. They're all stiff and tired from the shearing.

"It's like a family," says Susie.

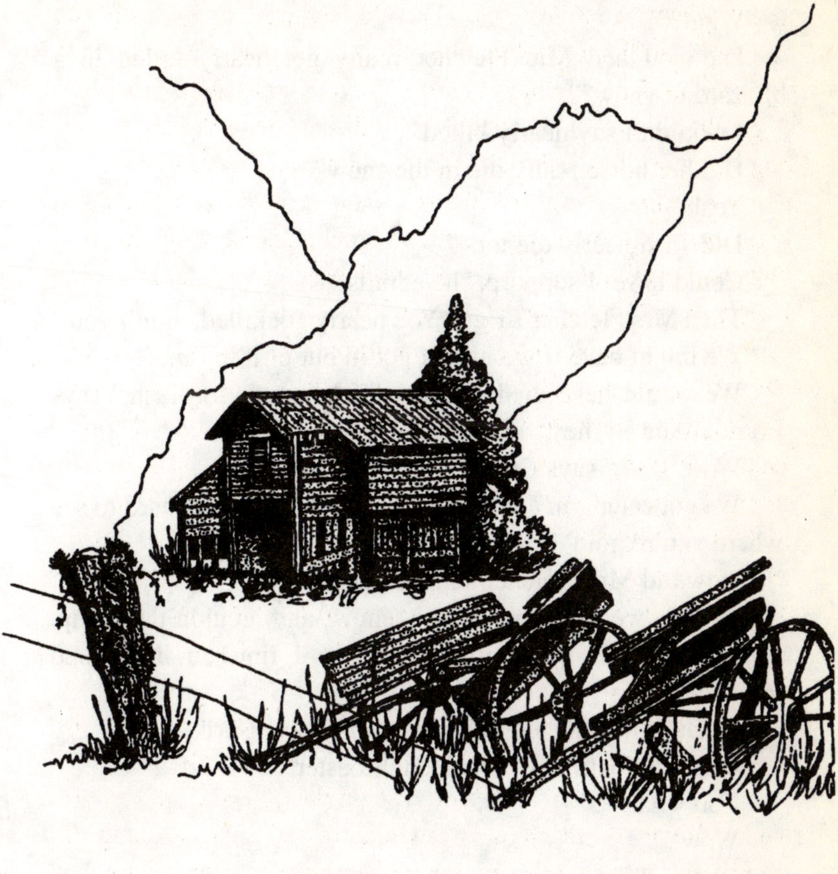

They look around at each other.

"So it is," says Lorna.

The Doughroaster grunts and looks back into the fire. The others go on with what they were doing.

"Dad?" says Susie.

"What?"

"Did you and Mrs Fletcher really get nearly killed in a blizzard of snow?"

"I wouldn't say nearly killed."

"Did her horse really die in the snow?"

"Yeah."

"Did Tash nearly die too?"

"Could have, I suppose," he admits.

"Then Mrs Fletcher's right. You nearly got killed, didn't you."

"We might have if we hadn't got in out of it in time."

"We would have died out there if it wasn't for Tash," says Lorna. "And Barney," she adds.

"Wow, Dad," says Chris. "What happened?"

"We got caught in a snowstorm, that's all. Its a bit hard to see where you're goin' in them things sometimes."

"How did Mrs Fletcher's horse get killed?"

"It just went down in the snow and couldn't get up. It was spent. It was going to die so I finished it off and left it there."

"What do you mean, finished it off?" says Chris.

"Cut its throat," says The Doughroaster.

"You what!"

"Wow!"

"Barney!"

"Daddy!"

All at once.

"It was the only way I could save it from dyin' slow," says The Doughroaster.

"How *could you,* though?"

"Y' have to be able to be a bit hard sometimes. It's hard country this."

"Barney, you never told me that," says Lorna, still a bit shocked.

"Sometimes things don't need sayin' at the time," says The Doughroaster. "You were pretty fond of that horse."

"Oh Mrs Fletcher," says Susie. She crosses to sit on the arm of her chair, giving her father a reproachful look.

It's tough on Doughroasters sometimes.

"It's all right, love," says Lorna. "Your father did the right thing."

"That's right," says Derek. "He had to do it."

"Glad it wasn't me, all the same," says Chris.

"How did all this happen, anyway?" asks Derek.

So Lorna tells what The Doughroaster reckons is a rather dramatised version of their adventure in the snow.

"Wow, in the bath!" says Chris.

"This must be a very dangerous place to live," says Susie.

"How close was it really, Dad?" asks Derek.

"As close as you'd want to get," says The Doughroaster, "but you could get into just as much trouble in the river at home. If you know what you're doin' this kind of country's no more dangerous than any other. Just a bit harder, that's all."

The truck with the last of their bales of wool leaves as The Hog and Tommy arrive in the Doubleburn ute.

"Shearing early, eh Doughroaster," says The Hog.

"Yeah. Thought we'd get it over and done with."

The Doughroaster introduces The Hog and Tommy to Derek

and Chris. They've dropped in to see if he wants anything from town. He doesn't, but by the time The Hog and Tommy leave both Derek and Chris are intrigued.

"What's this Doughroaster bit, Dad?"

"It's just a bit of a nickname."

"How come?"

"Well, when I first came round here I was cooking for a mustering gang on the place next door, and . . ."

"You? Cooking?"

"That's a joke!"

"No wonder they call you The Doughroaster!"

"They call all the cooks that round here," he says.

"Doughroaster, eh!"

"There's no need to get carried away. It's just a bit of a nickname."

"A good one though, eh! Especially for you!" says Chris.

"What's it worth not to tell them up home, Dad?" says Derek.

"You'd better bloody not!"

"Don't worry, only joking."

He's sitting around in the house with the boys the next day.

"Where's Susie?" says Derek.

"Outside somewhere with The Doughroastress," says Chris without looking up from his book.

"You don't want to let her hear you call her that," warns The Doughroaster.

He's a bit hacked-off about this. He's been imagining that the Doughroaster name will be left behind when he leaves here, but now it looks as though it might travel ahead of him and be waiting at home when he gets there. Instead of calling him Dad, Chris has started calling him Doughad. No respect, the young people these days.

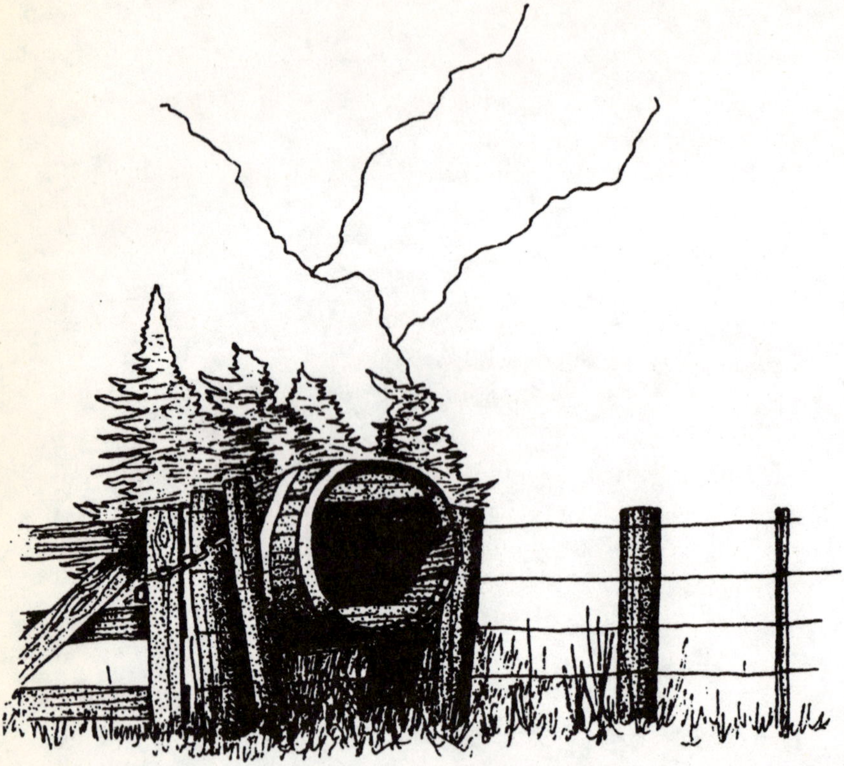

ELEVEN

SHOWDOWN AT BULLOCK CREEK

Derek wants to get home to the farm and his fiancee, and Susie has to go back to school, but Chris doesn't have to leave here yet. And he doesn't want to.

"How about I stay on and give you a hand here?" he suggests to The Doughroaster.

"There's nothing I can't handle on my own now, thanks all the same."

"Aw, come on, Dad. They don't need me up home just now. I could stay on here for a while, couldn't I?"

"You'd have to ask Lorna. If she says it's okay, it'll be alright, I suppose."

Chris dashes off to find Lorna, and says to her, "Dad wants me to stay on for a while and help him, if it's alright with you."

"Of course it's alright with me," she says. "You're more than welcome, Chris."

Chris gives her a hug. "Thanks, mate!"

And he runs off to find The Doughroaster again.

"She says it's okay!"

"Right, you can start by bringing the ute across and taking a couple of loads of this firewood up to the house. And you'd better stick the ute back on the other side of the river when you've done that. The weather looks like it's closing in again. Then you can get stuck into diggin' us a new rubbish hole."

Derek and Susie are leaving Clinton on the eleven-thirty bus to Christchurch in the morning, and this is after dinner in the evening.

"When do you think you'll be coming home, Dad?" asks Derek.

"Well the year's not up till Febr'y," says The Doughroaster.

"Oh forget the stupid year!" says Susie. "We'd rather have you at home with us than any silly farm."

Derek and Chris both nod.

"Okay," says The Doughroaster. "I don't mind coming back, but I still want to stick to our original deal. You boys run the farm at a profit for a year and you keep it. All I want is that forty acres across the river."

"There's no need for that," says Derek. "We can all work together."

"No we can't," says The Doughroaster.

"Why?" says Derek.

"Because I don't want to."

"Why, Daddy?" says Susie. "What's wrong with us?"

"Nothing, Sweetie," he tells her. "I just want to do my own things, that's all."

"You don't want us, do you," she says. "You've got sick of us – just like Mummy." She starts to cry and sob. Lorna goes to sit beside her, pulling a handkerchief out of her sleeve.

The Doughroaster looks at Derek. "Looks a bit that way to us," says Derek.

The Doughroaster looks at Chris. Chris nods with the corners of his mouth pulled down hard.

"Bloody tripe!" says The Doughroaster.

"Don't swear," says Lorna.

There's a pause while Susie's tears run down.

"Okay, Dad," says Derek. "You tell us, then."

"I – don't want to talk about it in front of Mrs Fletcher,"

fumbles The Doughroaster. "It's not her problem."

Lorna looks at him. "My problem wasn't yours when you offered to help me run the station through the winter without any pay, Barney," she says. "And my problem wasn't yours in the snow that day . . ."

These pauses are getting to The Doughroaster. He's not much good at these sort of consultations.

"Well – "

"Come on, Dad!" says Chris.

"Well – I'm a farmer," says The Doughroaster, as though that explains everything.

"What's that got to do with it?"

"I'm not a child-rearer. When your mother took off I didn't know what the hell to do with you kids except keep clothes on your backs and food in your bellies and get you educated, and that's what I've been doing."

"So?" says Chris.

"Well it's time you blokes were weaned. I'm good at what I do, but I'm not good at what you do. I don't want to have to adjust to what you're good at. I've done my bit on that farm. It needs to be run your way now. I'd only send it bankrupt, you know that, you've been telling me often enough."

"But what about you? What do you want to do?" says Chris.

"I want to build myself a shack on my forty acres and see if I can run a flock of purebred merinos on that country, that's all."

"Why merinos?" says Derek.

"Because I happen to like 'em. They're good eating."

"What about me?" says Susie.

"Don't you worry, Sweetie," says The Doughroaster. "I'll be there any time any of you need me. Once you kids realise you can get along without me you won't need to. It's the same as weaning stock, the way I figure it.'

"They're not cattle, Barney," says Lorna. "They're people!"

"I'm a bloody farmer," says The Doughroaster.

"Don't swear," says Lorna.

"I'll buy that, Dad," says Derek. "But why didn't you just tell us all this, without all the separation and that?"

"I've been trying to tell you for years, but we just end up arguin'. We needed putting in different paddocks for a while. Now you know YOU can do it. YOU can get on with it."

"What about me and Jean getting married?"

"What about it?"

"You haven't said anything about it."

"What do you want me to say?"

"Well – do you approve?"

"Does it make any difference if I approve or not?"

"Of course it does, Dad!" says Chris.

"Okay then, I approve."

They can all see it's the best they're going to get out of The Doughroaster on this matter at the moment.

"Then we can go ahead and plan the wedding for mid December,' says Derek.

"Okay, I'll be finished here by then."

"We finish up here on December the first," says Lorna, "but Barney can get away any time he likes."

"I think I'll see it out," says The Doughroaster. "There's a bit to be done here yet. I don't want to leave the job unfinished."

Chris has moved over to stand by the calendar on the wall. "December the first is a Wednesday," he says. "You could be up home by the fifth, driving it in the ute. That's a Saturday."

"Then we can arrange the wedding any time after the eighth," says Derek.

"Sure," says The Doughroaster.
"That's a Tuesday," calls out Chris.
"Except for one thing," says Derek.
"What?" says Chris.
"That's last year's calendar!"

Lorna laughs, The Doughroaster's kids laugh, and then The Doughroaster himself starts to laugh. And somehow during the moments when everyone's laughing free The Doughroaster and his family become united in a way they never knew before.

Next morning The Doughroaster leaves Chris to butcher two wethers while he and Lorna take Derek and Susie in to the bus. Susie's looking very cuddly in the homespun pullover Lorna's been knitting for her. Even Derek gives her a hug when she turns on a few tears as they're getting on the bus. "December the fifth," says Derek to The Doughroaster.

"I'll be home round then," says The Doughroaster.

And when the bus leaves The Doughroaster and the widow are standing in the same place they were a month ago, waiting for The Doughroaster's family to arrive. It's been a big month.

They do a bit of shopping and then head for home in silence. Then Lorna says, "You're a lucky man, Barney."

"How do you make that out?" he says.

"Your children, they're lovely."

"They're not children any more."

"They're lovely," she says again.

"They coulda turned out worse, I suppose."

"You're terribly hard on them, Barney. You're all they've got, you know."

"If they start thinkin' that, we've all had it," says The Doughroaster.

Lorna gives up and starts opening the mail as he drives on.

"Barney!"

"What?"

"The wool cheque, it's come through! It's been paid into my bank account!"

"How much?"

"Forty-eight thousand, six hundred and fifty-four dollars."

"That'll come in handy," he says. "We'll have to give the boys a few bucks for helping shear them."

"You ought to keep the rest of it, Barney," says Lorna.

"We can sort that out when your money for the station comes through. I don't really want that much"

"You've earned every cent of it," she says.

There's not much to do on Bullock Creek now. The Doughroaster and Chris ride the easy stuff and shift a bit of stock here and there. Riding back down Boundary Creek in the afternoon of a warm sunny day, Chris says, "You know, Dad, this country kind of grows on you, doesn't it."

The Doughroaster looks across at his son, "As long as you respect it, this country can make a man out of you."

"In what way?"

"You'd have to do it to find out."

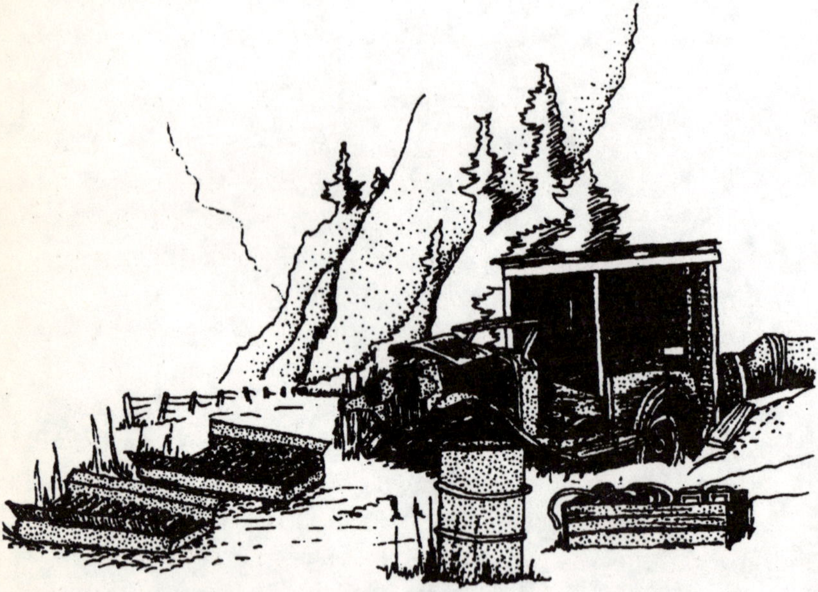

TWELVE

MIRACLE AT BULLOCK CREEK

Bullock Creek begins to take on a new atmosphere. Truckloads of mining equipment arrive and get stacked in the tussock along the roadsides across the river. Framework, pumps, conveyor-belts, pipes, winches – the dismantled parts of the big gold-separating plant The Doughroaster saw in that flash of light in the Mangatane implement shed that night. A big Hitachi digger arrives on a transporter, then a front-end loader, a wheel-tractor, then a big bulldozer.

Two men called Steve, the foreman, and The Relic, a little old bloke who's been gold-mining and whitebaiting all his life, are staying on Mangatane and driving over each day to work on assembling the plant. The Doughroaster's heard that it's cost them a million-and-a-half dollars to get the outfit to this stage, but figures like that are beyond his imagination.

The next manager on Bullock Creek is going to be Steve, who's in charge of the operation. About thirty, slight, fair and educated in a university. More at home in a four-wheel-drive than on a horse, his handpiece is a welding-torch, his knowledge is mechanical, his muck is oil and grease. A new generaton is moving into the back-country, with skills unknown to The Doughroaster. This is the day of computers and hydraulics. Helicopters and trail-bikes are their horses and dogs. Machines and money are their gods. Aeroplanes that carry hundreds of people at once, and young men and women who can play complicated video-games but can't tell one end of an animal from the other.

The Doughroaster resents the idea of people being able to stand on the top of a mountain without ever having been able to climb up there. Seems like cheating somehow.

Chris has been hanging around over at the gold-plant and now Steve has offered him a job. He's always been good with his hands and his smile, Chris.

"Do you know who you'll be working for?" says The Doughroaster.

"Someone called Knight. I've met him. He came over yesterday to see how we were getting on."

"He's a friend of Barney's," says Lorna.

"What's he like to work for?" asks Chris.

"Jake's okay," says The Doughroaster. "He just needs keeping an eye on."

"Why?"

"He's a bit inclined to let himself get carried away with his own importance, that's all."

Strange metallic sounds on Bullock Creek, as the men across the river hammer and weld and cut and bolt the parts of the plant together. The hopper, the revolving screen, the banks of riffles, the conveyor-belt for the tailings, water pumps, diesel motors – all set up on two big steel skids. If you didn't know what it was you'd never guess from looking at it.

Then one day Jake comes over to the house on the tractor and you can tell by his smile that he wants something.

"What can I do for you, Jake?" says The Doughroaster.

"We're ready to try out the rig, and we want to start up the far end of Miner's Flat and work our way towards here. I know we don't take over here until December, but if we could just set our gear up and get it working it'd save us a lot of time and money."

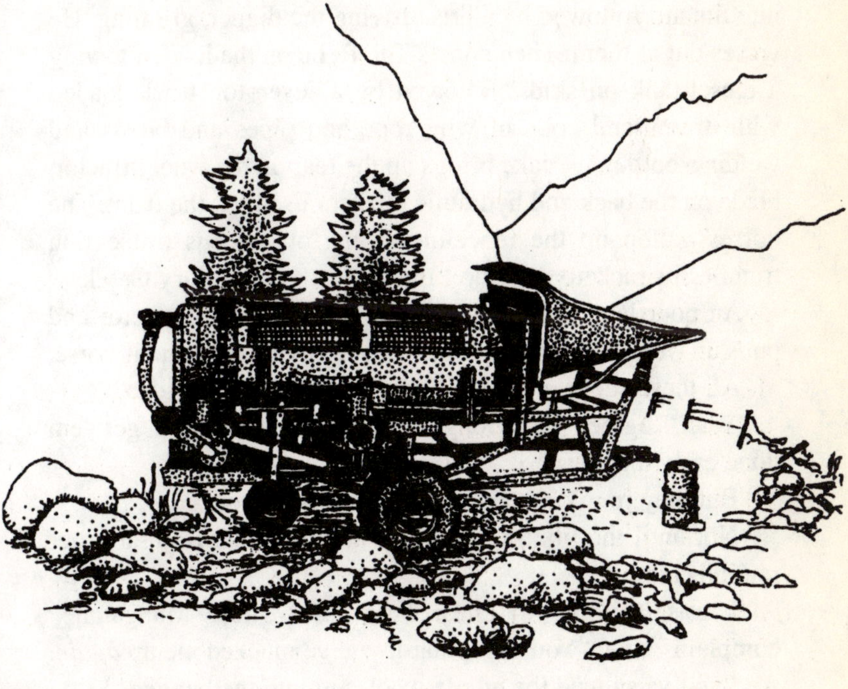

"Long as you don't disturb the stock," The Doughroaster tells him.

"Thanks, Doughroaster."

The big bulldozer pushes a track through the heaps of stones and scrub. The Doughroaster and Lorna watch as the bulldozer drags the gold-plant across the river and past the old woolshed and out across the holding-paddock. A strange monster in this landscape, crawling along, roaring and blowing diesel-smoke into the air, followed by Chris, driving the digger, grinning. He waves out to them. Then comes The Relic on the loader, towing a diesel-tank on skids, followed by a seven-ton truck loaded with drums and coils of wire rope and pipes and boxes and welding-bottles... Jake brings up the rear on the wheel-tractor, blade on the back and hydraulic bucket raised out the front. The horses gallop up the fenceline as the outrageous procession trundles its racketty way up Miner's Flat to Boundary Creek.

An hour later Jake comes bouncing back on his tractor and pulls up with an angry jerk beside The Doughroaster on his horse.

"All these sheep are shorn!" he says. "What's the idea?"

"Yeah," agrees The Doughroaster. "Thought we'd get 'em done early this year."

"But they're my bloody sheep! That's my wool."

"Not until the first of December it isn't," The Doughroaster reminds him.

"I wasn't going to shear here till I shear Mangatane,' complains Jake. "You old bastard, you've mucked me up *again*. And you've swiped the whole wool-clip into the bargain!"

"You farm your way, I'll farm mine," says The Doughroaster. "I'm the manager of this station. You're lucky I've let you on here at all. You wouldn't let me on your place, remember."

"It didn't stop you going on my place though, did it?"

"That's the difference. I *can* stop you."

Jake thumps the steering-wheel of his tractor in exasperation, "If you're not off this place by the first of December I'm going to personally throw you off. I mean it. And if I ever see you around here again, so help me, I'll bloody *shoot you*!"

"In the meantime you'd better not upset me too much, me old cobber," says The Doughroaster. "I could hold up your operation for three weeks yet."

"You think you're pretty smart, don't you?" says Jake.

"I'm no smarter than you are," The Doughroaster tells him. "Your trouble is that you're greedy as well as smart."

The Doughroaster rides off across the tussock and he hears Jake start his tractor behind him and turn it round and bounce away up his bulldozed track towards Boundary Creek.

Two hours later Chris arrives back at the station on foot and comes down where The Doughroaster's unsaddling his horse.

"Hell, Dad. What have you done to Jake?" he says.

"Why, what's wrong with him now?"

"You should have seen him. He came back out there and started calling you a thieving old bastard and stuff like that. And when I told him to lay off talking about my old man like that he freaked-out. I thought he was going to throw a fit!"

"What'd he do?" grins The Doughroaster.

"He went round hitting things with his hat and shouting, 'Now I've got the old bastard's bloody *son* working for me!'"

"Did he give you the sack?"

"Not exactly, but I thought I'd better get out of there before he got violent. What have you *done* to him?"

"Nothin' much," says The Doughroaster. "He tried to put one across me a while back, but I put one across him instead, and he doesn't like it."

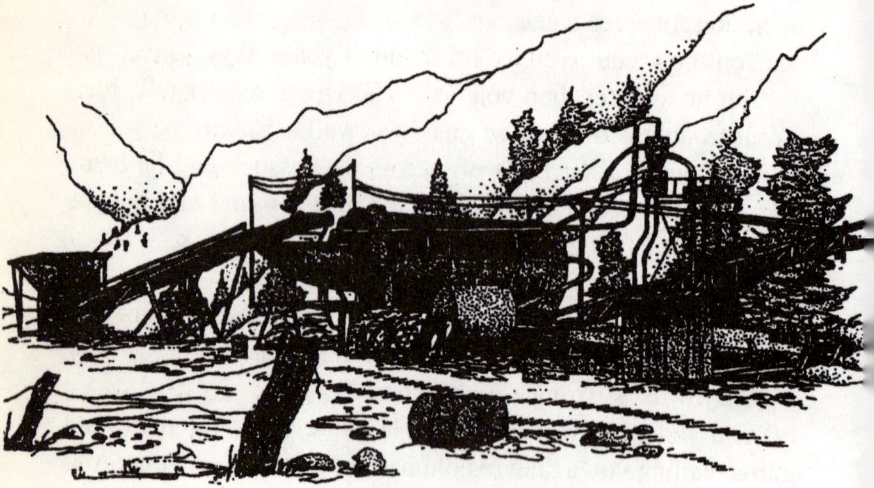

"You're telling me he doesn't like it. Wow!"

"Jake'll settle down. He gets a bit excited at times, but he knows what side his bread's buttered on."

"I sure hope so. I'm a bit scared to go back out there."

"Just turn up tomorrow as if nothing's happened, and pull your weight," advises The Doughroaster. "Good workers are hard to get around here."

Next morning Jake arrives with his men in the Land Cruiser and stops to pick up Chris without looking sideways at The Doughroaster leaning on the gate. Later that day, from high on a ridge, The Doughroaster hears the diesel motors roaring in Boundary Creek, and that night there's excitement when they drop Chris off at the homestead an hour after dark. They've operated the plant for two-and-a-half hours and then had to stop to fix something, and while they were doing that The Relic and Chris washed up nearly three ounces of gold. Very promising.

This is it. The Doughroaster can leave here now. He's been waiting to see how Jake would handle finding out he's ripped off the wool clip. He's got all he wants and he's done just about all he needs to. Now it's just a matter of waiting to make sure Lorna gets her cheque for the station.

It's obvious that Chris is going to want to stay on here. He's right into gold recovery, and already indispensable to the team. He talks about nothing else. The Doughroaster privately likes the idea of leaving a son of his in this back country. The miners are going to move into the homestead when Lorna and The Doughroaster move out. The Culprit's going to cook for them and they've already got some of their gear stacked in the spare room off the veranda and in the woolshed.

They're leaving on Tuesday and this is Friday. Lorna's had a phone call from her bank. Her cheque for the station will be processed early next week.

"I get a hundred and twenty thousand, after they deduct the mortgage money," she tells The Doughroaster.

"That's one thing off your mind," he says.

"It's been the main thing on my mind for more than three years, and now it's over. I've got you to thank for all this, Barney. I would have given it up if it wasn't for you."

"I don't think you'd have quit," he says. "But you'd probably have lost a fair bit of stock, one way and another."

"Just think of it, Barney. It's over at last. I can hardly believe it.!"

"It'll sink in." He grins at her excitement.

Most of Lorna's gear is already packed in boxes and wool packs and waits on the woolshed ramp for the carrier to take over to Mataura to her family's home. There's nothing else they have to do so they saddle their horses and ride out to have a look at the gold-plant working. They travel on the new bulldozed road and get there in half the usual time.

The operation is in full swing. A big dam filled with water pumped up out of Boundary Creek is being recycled through the roaring rumbling complications of machinery. A steel ribbed monster, two hundred feet long and thirty feet high, its hide scaled with ladders and walkways and handrails, a thundering diesel heart and wide-open throat swallowing up ton after ton of rock and gravel and digesting it in its churning, dripping stomach and pouring the tailings out in long heaps to be levelled away by the tractor. All this activity and noise and disturbance of the land in search of half a teacupful of golden bile, if they're lucky.

And so Bullock Creek finally has what The Doughroaster reckoned would suit the conditions here; something cold-blooded that eats rock. It's as close to being a miracle as anything he's ever seen. Sitting on his horse watching it, he realises that he's been borrowing a piece of time out of his past, a nostalgic journey into the last traces of a disappearing style of life no one wants to know about any more.

And now it's time to return to the present. They wave to Chris grinning on the digger and then turn and ride back towards the homestead on the old horse-track. The roaring of the diesels fades away behind them and they ride along enjoying the silence. Then Lorna says, "Tell me something, Barney."

"What?"

"You say this place is uneconomical as a farm."

"That's right. There's no way you could make a high-country place this size pay these days."

"Then what made you offer to manage it for me?"

"Needed something to do, I suppose. A man must'a been mad."

"But the station *has* made a profit since you've been running it, and that's been through that terrible winter."

"You'd never get away with it again," he says.

"What do you mean?"

"Too hard to explain," he says, "but you just couldn't keep it up."

"Kevin would have loved to see Bullock Creek succeed. It was his dream."

It's the first time she's mentioned her dead husband since the day he started working for her.

"He was dreaming all right,' says The Doughroaster. "If there was only two sheep on this place one of them would quite likely starve to death."

They ride along in silence for a while and then Lorna says,

"Well it's all finished for us here now."

"Yeah, I know."

"What will you do, Barney?"

"Go back up north and start building a place to live on my forty acres across the river, I suppose. The boys seem to have the farm pretty well sorted out, but they'll need a hand now and then, especially with Chris away working down here. If he gets this gold-mining in his blood we mightn't see him again up there. What about you?"

"Oh I'll probably buy myself a house somewhere. A small one. After that I'll have to wait and see."

They ride along in silence for another while, and then The Doughroaster says, "Just thought of something."

"What's that?"

"I'm going to need a good doughroaster on my place up north."

"What are you paying?"

"Nothing, unless the price of wool goes up."

"What's the food like?"

"Mutton and spuds, if there is any."

"What about accommodation?"

"You sleep in a shed and cook over an open fire until we get the house built."

"How do you apply for the job?"

"In person, to the boss."

"I'd like to put in for it."

"I don't know. Have you had any experience?"

"Yep."

"Can you handle living in an isolated place?"

"Yep."

"Flooded rivers?"

"Yep."
"Snow?"
"Yep."
"Mud?"
"Love it!"
"Can you handle other people's kids?"
"Depends."
"I might give you a week's trial."
"What about a year?"
"A year's a long time," says The Doughroaster.
"I gave you more than a week's trial when you came to work for me," she says.
"Okay. You've got a year's trial as doughroaster on Carter's forty acres in the Taranaki."
"I accept the position."
"There's only one condition."
"What's that?"
"The doughroaster's not allowed to feed the boss's dog when he's not around."
"Of course not. A doughroaster could get the sack for doing a thing like that!"

They can't see each other because The Doughroaster's riding a few yards ahead, but they're both grinning fit to bust. Each of them has been wondering about all that. And The Doughroaster's dog trots along in front.

Next day the gold rig is idle, waiting for spare parts. The Doughroaster rides the gelding over to Doubleburn for the last time. The Hog will ride him now. Chris and Lorna follow in the ute. Everyone's home at Doubleburn. The Doughroaster's been around here for the best part of a year and this is the first time he's actually met The Hog's wife, Maisy, and the two Nathan boys, home for the weekend.

Chris and the Nathan boys and Tommy disappear, knee deep in dogs, to hunt some wild pigs that have been rooting up the top flats. Ross opens bottles of beer for The Hog, The Doughroaster and himself, and Nancy pours glasses of wine for the ladies. And they toast the sale of Bullock Creek.

By the time the boys return with a big sow and a young boar, Nancy is tinkling on the piano in the livingroom, and suddenly a party is happening. They sing songs The Doughroaster hasn't heard for years: *Irene Goodnight, Danny Boy, On Top of Old Smoky, Way Down Upon, A Swanee River.*

The Yellow Rose of Texas. Cool Water. Molly Malone . . . Lorna's got a beautiful singing voice.

They sing until nearly midnight. They have a toast-and cheese type of supper, and after prolonged and rather sloppy farewells, they drive away.

"Where did you learn to sing like that?" The Doughroaster asks Lorna.

"In church choirs, mostly."

"Might've guessed."

It's Tuesday. The ute's loaded. They take a last look around to see if they've left anything behind, then The Doughroaster and Lorna get in and drive across the river for the last time, with Tash's head sticking up among the stuff on the back. As they turn out onto the road Jake's Land Cruiser is coming towards them. It's Jake and The Culprit. They wave briefly as they pass, and disappear out of each other's lives, no doubt to Jake's great relief.

"There's only one thing I can't figure out about that bloke," says The Doughroaster.

"Is there?" says Lorna.

"I can't figure out why he keeps that creepy bloody Culprit around him."

"Don't swear. I'd have thought it was quite obvious."

"It's not obvious to me. The Culprit's a real sneaky hunk of work. You have to watch him like a hawk."

"Isn't Jake something like that himself?" says Lorna, shaking out knitting. "He wouldn't see that much wrong with The Culprit, would he?"

The Doughroaster looks across at her and can't help breaking out in a bit of a grin. They drive on for a bit and then he says, "I'll tell you about me and Jake one of these days."

"I've always known there was something funny going on between you two," says Lorna. "What was it all about?"

"It's a long story."

"It's a long journey."

And as they drive away from Bullock Creek towards a new and easier life, The Doughroaster tells Lorna the bits she doesn't know about his last adventure in the high-country. He wouldn't like to have to do all that every winter, but he wouldn't have missed it for anything.